Hertfordshire
COUNTY COUNCIL
Community Information

10|4

609.41
HUDSON Kenneth.

Please renew/return this item by the last date shown.

So that your telephone call is charged at local rate, please call the numbers as set out below:

	From Area codes 01923 or 020:	From the rest of Herts:
Renewals:	01923 471373	01438 737373
Enquiries:	01923 471333	01438 737333
Minicom:	01923 471599	01438 737599

L32   www.hertsdirect.org

D0540407

CAMBRIDGE AIR SURVEYS

INDUSTRIAL HISTORY FROM THE AIR

CAMBRIDGE AIR SURVEYS

Edited by DAVID R. WILSON

CURATOR IN AERIAL PHOTOGRAPHY, UNIVERSITY OF CAMBRIDGE

D. KNOWLES and J. K. S. ST JOSEPH

Monastic Sites from the Air
(out of print)

M. W. BERESFORD and J. K. S. ST JOSEPH

Medieval England
An Aerial Survey

E. R. NORMAN and J. K. S. ST JOSEPH

The Early Development of Irish Society
The evidence of Aerial Photography

S. S. FRERE and J. K. S. ST JOSEPH

Roman Britain from the Air

Industrial history from the air

KENNETH HUDSON

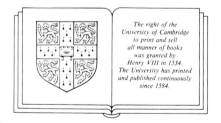

The right of the
University of Cambridge
to print and sell
all manner of books
was granted by
Henry VIII in 1534.
The University has printed
and published continuously
since 1584.

CAMBRIDGE UNIVERSITY PRESS

CAMBRIDGE
LONDON   NEW YORK   NEW ROCHELLE
MELBOURNE   SYDNEY

Published by the Press Syndicate of the University of Cambridge
The Pitt Building, Trumpington Street, Cambridge CB2 1RP
32 East 57th Street, New York, NY 10022, USA
10 Stamford Road, Oakleigh, Melbourne 3166, Australia

© Cambridge University Press 1984

First published 1984

Printed in Great Britain by B.A.S. Printers Ltd, Over Wallop

Library of Congress catalogue card number: 84–7035

British Library Cataloguing in Publication Data
Hudson, Kenneth
Industrial history from the air.–
(Cambridge air surveys)
1. Industrial archaeology – Great Britain
I. Title
609(.41   T26.G7

ISBN 0 521 25333 0

BO

Contents

Contents

Photographs described in the text

For those photographs which have serial numbers, these are given in the captions.

FIGURES IN THE TEXT

Preface

The usefulness of aerial photography as a research tool has long been recognised by British archaeologists whose field of study lies within the prehistoric, Roman, Saxon and medieval periods, where archaeology means primarily excavations. Viewed from above, the landscape reveals historical secrets whose existence is hidden from scholars whose insight is limited to what can be discovered by walking over the ground. Photographs taken from the air put already known sites into a fuller and more meaningful context. They make it possible, in M. W. Bereford's excellent phrase 'to comprehend detail as a unity'[1]. The influence of man on the landscape begins to make sense. One comes to understand that 'topography is a human creation, or rather a creation of men struggling with and using natural resources'[2].

But topography, like archaeology, has no time limits. The modification of the landscape to serve human needs and wishes is a continuous process and those stages which belong to the twentieth century are no less worthy of study than those which characterise the second or the fourteenth. It would have been perfectly reasonable to have called the present book, the latest in the series of Cambridge Air Surveys, *Industrial Archaeology from the Air* – industrial archaeology is now accepted as a serious and helpful branch of historical research – but it seemed wiser, after careful consideration, to prefer *Industrial History from the Air*. There were two main reasons for coming to this decision. The first was political. Tradition dies hard and there are many scholars who remain to be convinced that a factory, a dock or an aerodrome can be brought within the canon of archaeology, although they are happy enough to regard such material as useful historical evidence. The second reason for choosing 'History', rather than 'Archaeology', was that, on many sites, one is faced with a continuum which includes, at its contemporary end, buildings and equipment which are no more than five or ten years old. One day they will, like all man-made creations, be entitled to the label 'archaeology', but it would be forcing the issue somewhat to suggest that this time has already arrived. So, since aerial photography has the enormous advantage of allowing one to see a long span of industrial development within the same focus, *Industrial History from the Air* appeared more likely to turn readers' thoughts in the right direction and to nip misconceptions and prejudices in the bud. But there is no reason for industrial archaeologists to feel that the author has deserted their cause. The title is intended to widen the public for the book and, indeed, to emphasise that industrial archaeology exists to serve industrial history.

Most of the photographs used as illustrations in the following pages are from the archives of the Cambridge Committee for Aerial Photography. Nearly all the exceptions fall into one of two categories – early aerial photographs, taken before Cambridge began to form its collections and used here for comparative purposes, and photographs shot from the ground and included to illustrate the difference between this kind of visual documentation and what can be obtained by means of aerial photography.

References

1. *Medieval England: an Aerial Survey*, 1958, p. 4.
2. *Ibid.*. p. 6.

Acknowledgements

My especial gratitude is due to David Wilson, Curator in Aerial Photography in the University of Cambridge, and General Editor of Cambridge Air Surveys. From the moment when the book was first mentioned as a possibility until its completion he has provided invaluable help in shaping and steering my work. If the present book is a not unworthy companion to its predecessors in the series, the result is due primarily to him. He has devoted a great deal of time, first, to locating prints which already existed within the University's huge collection of aerial photographs and, secondly, to taking new photographs of subjects which I was particularly anxious to see represented in the book. He and his colleagues have made my visits to Cambridge exceedingly pleasant and fruitful.

I should also like to thank the many people who have helped me with specialised local enquiries and who have made available information without which the satisfactory interpretation of the photographs would have been extremely difficult. Colin Sorensen, of the Museum of London, was most generous of his time in educating me about the history of London's docks, and, for material relating to Liverpool Docks, I am greatly indebted to Janet Smith, of Liverpool Record Office, and to R. E. Davies, of the Mersey Docks and Harbour Company.

Jonathan Bryant, of Chatterley Whitfield Mining Museum, and Frank Atkinson, of Beamish, gave me much-appreciated help in connection with the history of coal-mining; Barrie Hedges, of Blue Circle Industries, provided detailed information about the manufacture of cement, and Suzanne Dix, of the London Brick Company, performed a similar kindly service in connection with the brick industry. For quarrying, I am very grateful to M. W. H. McKay, of Foster Yeoman Ltd., and to P. Askins of the Amey Roadstone Corporation. Alan Joiner, of BL Cars, guided me through the complicated history of Morris and British Leyland at Cowley. Alison Palmer and Alan Timbrell, of the British Airports Authority, were very helpful in equipping me with photographs and historical information concerning Gatwick Airport, and A. E. Gunn was extremely generous with help and advice in connection with Shoreham Airport. For the history of the petroleum industry, I have to thank especially D. M. Hunt, of Shell UK, and Miss V. McGregor, of the Esso Petroleum Company, and for the development of the New Towns, Peter Rose, at Peterborough, Mrs C. Carr, at Telford, and several members of the staff of Cumbernauld Development Corporation. I have also received very useful assistance from Mrs V. Langworthy, of Derby Central Library, from the Cambridge Local Studies Library, and from T. S. A. Macquiban, Borough Archivist at Doncaster.

The story of Britain's industrial estates has been unreasonably neglected. In piecing it together and in relating it to the photographs I selected for this book, I should have experienced many problems without the generous assistance of the administration at Trafford Park, Gloucester and Slough, and of firms and individuals associated with the estates over a long period.

Michael Middleton, of the Civic Trust, has been closely concerned for many years with the problems of industrial dereliction and with the rehabilitation of the areas affected. Without his efforts, it would have been difficult to understand the scale of the problem and to appreciate the success of the efforts which have been made to solve it.

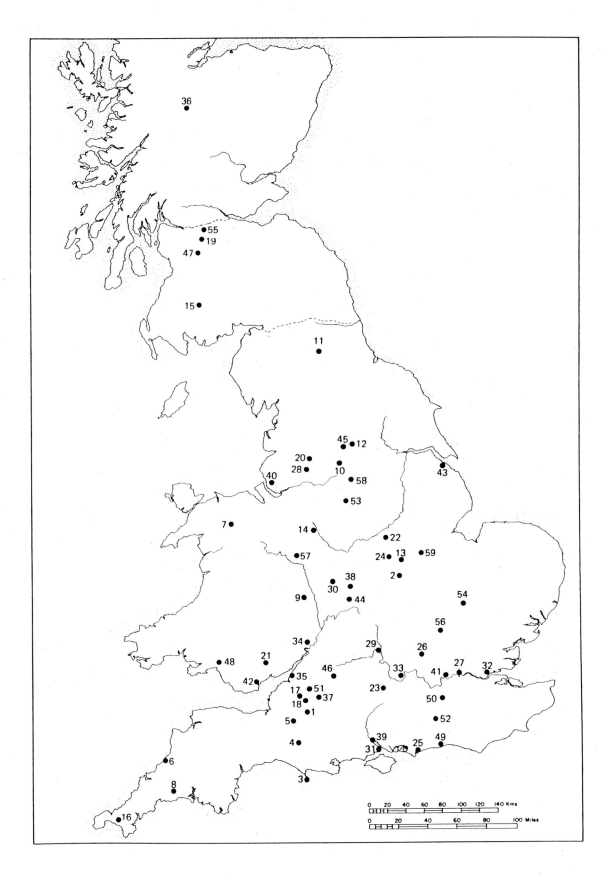

Key to location map

1 Blue Circle Cement works, Westbury, Wiltshire
2 Bedfordshire brickfield
3 Limestone quarries at Portland, Dorset
4 Hamdon Hill quarries, Somerset
5 Stone quarries of East Mendip, Somerset
6 Delabole slate quarry, Cornwall
7 Great Oakley slate quarry, Gwynedd
8 China-clay panorama, St Stephen-in-Brannel, Cornwall
9 Coal mines at Catherton Common, Shropshire
10 Iron mines at Bentley Grange, Emley, South Yorkshire
11 Lead mines near Forest, Co. Durham
12 Coal pits at Garforth, West Yorkshire
13 Mining subsidence near Little Addington, Northamptonshire
14 Chatterley Whitfield colliery, Tunstall, Staffordshire
15 Abandoned coal mine at Dalmellington, Strathclyde
16 Tin mining near St Hilary, Cornwall
17 Woollen mills at Bradford-on-Avon, Wiltshire
18 Trowbridge, Wiltshire
19 New Lanark, Strathclyde
20 Park Mill, Royton, Lancashire
21 British Nylon Spinners, Pontypool, Gwent
22 Pedigree Petfoods, Melton Mowbray, Leicestershire
23 Suttons of Reading, Berkshire
24 Weetabix, Burton Latimer, Leicestershire
25 Lec Refrigeration, Bognor Regis, West Sussex
26 Elstree film studios, Hertfordshire
27 Ford factory, Dagenham, Essex
28 Old Ford works, Trafford Park, Manchester, Greater Manchester
29 British Leyland works, Cowley, Oxfordshire
30 Fort Dunlop, Birmingham, West Midlands
31 Oil refining at Fawley, Hampshire
32 Lubricating oil at Shell Haven, Essex
33 Slough Trading Estate, Berkshire
34 Gloucester Trading Estate
35 River system in central Bristol, Avon
36 Caledonian Canal at Fort Augustus, Highland
37 Kennet and Avon locks, Devizes, Wiltshire
38 Crick tunnel, Northamptonshire
39 Southampton dock area, Hampshire
40 Liverpool docks, Merseyside
41 London docks
42 Cardiff docks, South Glamorgan
43 Grimsby docks, Humberside
44 Railway construction near Charwelton, Northamptonshire
45 Railway complex at Leeds, West Yorkshire
46 Railway workshops, Swindon, Wiltshire
47 Darvel, Strathclyde
48 Former tramroad at Tonna, West Glamorgan
49 Shoreham, West Sussex
50 Croydon Airport, Surrey
51 Whitchurch Airport, Avon
52 Gatwick, West Sussex
53 Creswell, Derbyshire
54 Bar Hill, Cambridgeshire
55 Cumbernauld, Strathclyde
56 Letchworth Garden City, Herfordshire
57 Telford, Shropshire
58 New Rossington, South Yorkshire
59 Peterborough, Cambridgeshire

Introduction: Industrial sites as seen from the air

'Industrial history', like 'industrial archaeology', is not an ideal term, but it is difficult to think of a better one. It is used here to describe the development of mining and quarrying, metal processing, transport and manufacturing over a period of approximately three hundred years. Not everyone would think of a canal, a windmill or a railway tunnel as 'industry', but if the word is taken in its older and broader sense of 'the state of being industrious', there is no problem. 'Industry', like agriculture and the building of towns and villages, forms part of man's efforts to control, tame and exploit the landscape and to earn a living from it. The fact that so many of these efforts have had regrettable, sometimes disastrous consequences is beside the point. The first duty of the historian is not to disapprove or to enthuse, but to document what has happened. He may well have a strong dislike of what previous generations have done or, more precisely, of the present results of past activity, but if he is to preserve his professional integrity, he must begin by assembling the evidence, by recording, describing and presenting what has survived.

In the case of industrial history, the relevant evidence is of four kinds: structures and ruins of structures – for our present purpose canals, railways, quarries and mines are all reckoned to be structures; machinery, tools and equipment used within the structure or in association with it; contemporary statements which have been written down in order to form a personal memoir; and the reminiscences of men and women who have been directly involved in a particular industry or workplace. These four constitute the first-hand industrial archive. None is more or less important than the others. All are required by the historian who is anxious to construct a full and fair picture of some aspect of the past; the absence of any one of them is almost certain to produce a distorted, unbalanced or misleading view of the achievements and attitudes of previous generations.

Aerial photography has a direct connection with only the first type of evidence, the structures, but it can often be of great assistance in arriving at a correct interpretation of the other three. This is mainly because of its usefulness in improving our awareness of context and scale. From the air, one can see how the separate pieces of the industrial jigsaw fit together and how they relate to their non-industrial surroundings. Broadly speaking, nothing looks the same from above as it does from the ground, a fact which has been realised for a long time in places where there were opportunities to climb a tower or a steep hill and to survey the district from the vantage point of a bird or of God. But such a possibility has always been exceptional, and most of the earth's surface could not be regarded in this way until first the balloon and then the aeroplane provided a mobile observation platform which could, at least theoretically, be used anywhere. For better or for worse, the God's-eye view had henceforth become available to mortals. The universal spying machine had arrived.

It is, of course, a matter for debate as to which is the 'real' or the most significant perspective, from the ground or from the air. As yet, human beings cannot fly unaided. They are equipped by nature to regard the earth more or less horizontally and their understanding of what is all around them is largely determined by this. The façades of buildings are considered to be more 'normal' than roofs and the patterning of man-made structures in the landscape is the one of which we are aware when we are walking, not when we are flying. The aerial view nearly always produces some degree of surprise or shock, simply because it is not the one we are used to. Aeroplane passengers, however experienced, rarely fail to find absorbing this unaccustomed view of London, Paris, the English Channel, or whatever the particular stretch of landscape spread out beneath them may be. To see familiar places from the air and to pick out landmarks is a pleasure all its own. Flying makes geography and topography real in a special way, but it would be absurd to claim that the world seen from the air is intrinsically any more real than the world seen from the ground. The roof of a building is neither more nor less real than its walls, but it is the aspect which is more frequently ignored by those who spend their time on the ground.

The surprise created by an aeroplane flight or

1

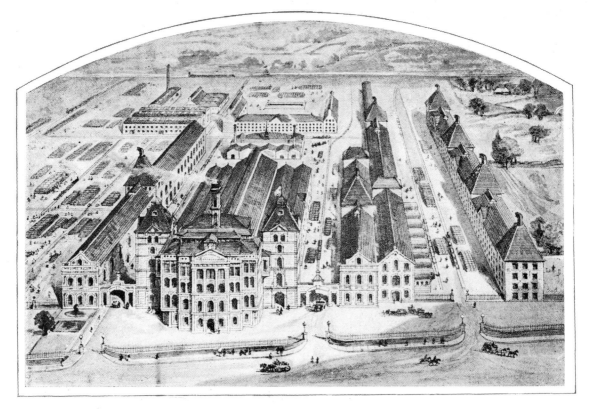

1 **The Anglo-Bavarian Brewery, Shepton Mallet, Somerset, 1880.** The bird's eye view, a foretaste of aerial photography, in which the artist is free to clean up and romanticise the site. From A. B. Gower, *A History of Shepton Mallet* (1880), facing p. 11.

by a photograph taken from the air can be very stimulating. It can also be unsettling. Nothing afterwards is quite the same as it used to be. Secrets have been uncovered, proportions changed, unsuspected beauties revealed, threats to the environment discovered. Perhaps the greatest change is the extent to which a landscape, especially an urban landscape, becomes dehumanised (see **2**, and cf. **3** and **108**). Wartime bomber crews were well aware of this. At 6,000 m or more above the target, they heard nothing and saw nothing of the destruction and suffering caused by the attack. They were aware of explosions and flames, but only as parts of a gigantic fireworks display. It took an almost impossible effort of the imagination to place oneself down below, at the receiving end of the bombs, in the strange alien world of observers on the ground.

But in one respect the situation is changing fast. In 1930, perhaps one in a thousand of the adult population in Britain had ever been up in an aeroplane. The figure now would probably be something like one in two. One consequence of this must be that it is now almost normal to have

seen the world from above and that the power of the aerial view to astonish has been much reduced. By the time they are thirty, most people, either at first or at second hand, have seen such a miracle so many times they know what the world looks like from this angle.

It was not always so. In the 1920s and 1930s, both passengers and operators were very conscious of the excitement and poetry of looking down on the world below and they were not ashamed to admit it. As one publication put it:

Life expands in an aeroplane. The traveller is a mere slave in a train, and, should he manage to escape from this particular yoke, the car and the ship present him with only limited horizons. Air travel, on the other hand, makes it possible for him to enjoy 'the solitary deserts of infinite space'. It allows him to look around him freely and at never-ending variety. The earth speeds by him with nothing hidden and full of surprises, with its clear waters, its peaceful forests, its welcoming villages and fields.[1]

One should remember, however, that, until the arrival of pressurised aircraft in the 1960s, airline passengers were accustomed to fly at altitudes of no more than 5,000–6,000 feet, from where it was

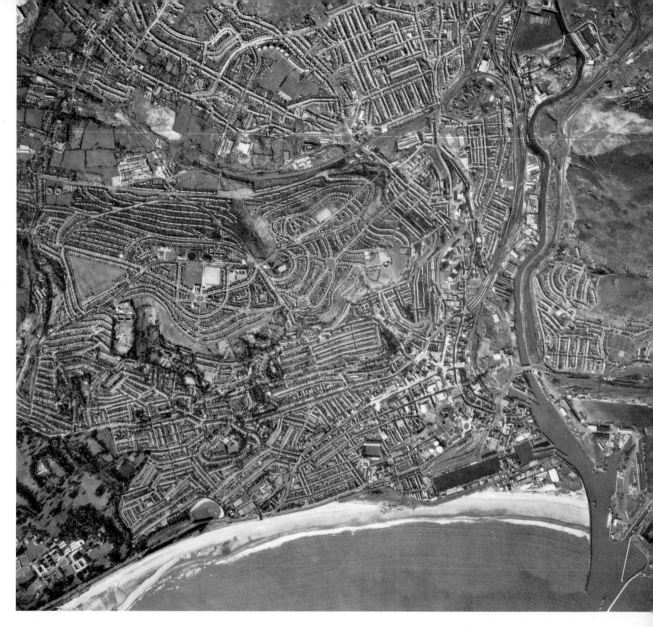

2 The dehumanised landscape. The photograph, looking vertically down, reveals patterns of housing in Swansea, with the docks in the bottom right-hand corner. From the air the rows of houses have become strings of beads, sequins sewn on a dress. This astonishing visual effect makes one forget, at least at a first glance, that one is looking down on human habitations. A photograph taken at an oblique angle is much less likely to have this result. It is the removal of the walls and the concentration on the roofs which causes the dehumanisation. Cambridge University Collection, RC8–N 194: October 1969. Scale 1:28,250.

possible to see the ground clearly for hours on end, whereas nowadays, at 30,000 feet and more, the view downwards is all too likely to be of nothing more than the cloud mass, with the earth becoming interesting only for a few minutes after take-off and before landing. It is no longer possible to write, as it was in 1936:

After leaving here we flew over some mountains which completely enclosed an enormous plateau, which is the natural habitat of lions, elephants, giraffes, zebras, gnus, gazelles, &c &c and buffalo. All except the lions we saw and I photographed and hope I got them in.[2]

Much amateur photography of this kind went on among the privileged people who travelled by air between the Wars, but it was only very rarely of industrial subjects. These were essentially a professional concern. The amateurs, on the whole, went for what was considered to be the more romantic and less workaday material and, mainly because of the equipment they used, their contribution to the history of aerial photography was not usually of a high standard.

Many remarkably good aerial photographs do survive from the 1920s and 1930s, however. Most

3

3 Dehumanisation forestalled. Housing estates in Telford, Shropshire. The contrast with **2** is striking. The patterning is nearly as remarkable, but the oblique view prevents the viewer from seeing it as pure pattern. The houses are unmistakably houses. Cambridge University Collection, BJT 69: July 1972.

of them are of ports and docks and of major industrial areas, commissioned by clients who had a direct interest in the subjects. If they are characterised by a certain sameness, and if few of them were published at the time, one needs to remember the extent to which the climate of industrial history has changed during the past quarter of a century. The difference has been brought about mainly by the activities and publications of a breed of people who did not exist until then, the industrial archaeologists. This very British type of enthusiast came into existence at a time when old factories and mills were being abandoned and demolished by the score, when historic machinery was being broken up and sold for its scrap value, and when the railway system was contracting. There was a great deal of industrial archaeology about, and much of it was under the immediate threat of destruction. The industrial archaeologists, a curiously mixed company of people, campaigned vigorously to save as many of these precious relics as possible and, in the process, found themselves under pressure to defend themselves, by explaining to an often incredulous

public why this or that building or piece of machinery was of cultural significance.

Over the same period, there has been a movement, greatly helped by radio and television, to collect and publish the reminiscences of elderly men and women, mainly of the working class. The movement has been dignified and to some extent formalised under the not altogether appropriate title of Oral History. Together, oral history and industrial archaeology have done much to broaden the concept of industrial history and, by doing so, to increase popular interest in it.

But all enthusiasms bring their own special dangers, much as all revolutions contain the germ of a new conservatism. The oral historians have often given the impression of regarding history preserved and transmitted by means of the spoken word as something more authentic, reliable and unprejudiced than history based on written sources. The industrial archaeologists have sometimes tended to claim some kind of historical superiority for the three-dimensional over the two-dimensional. They have also tended to display an unreasonable obsession with the cre-

4

4 The landscape purified by the camera. The area is at Landore, north of Swansea, and the photograph shows the dereliction caused by a century and a half of smelting. The waste-tips are sterile – nothing grows on them – and the smoke from the factory chimneys befouls the atmosphere and blights the vegetation in the immediate vicinity, although the smelters are sited so that the prevailing winds keep pollution mostly clear of the houses which lie off the bottom edge of the picture. The black-and-white picture has a soothing influence on the mind and the senses. A strongly working imagination is required in order to restore the unpleasantness of the scene. Cambridge University Collection, CZ 40: June 1949.

ations of the First Industrial Revolution, the period of steam, iron and railways, as against those of the Second, characterised by petroleum, aluminium and electricity.

It is important not to fall into similar traps so far as aerial photographs are concerned, although it is easy enough to do so. These photographs provide so much new understanding, so many new ideas and are frequently so exciting in themselves, that the temptation to say that what is seen from above has more meaning than what faces one on the ground often becomes very strong. It has, nevertheless, to be resisted. Just as industrial archaeology, like archaeology in general, is only an additional tool available to the historian, one more way of comprehending the past, so aerial photography is nothing more than a complement, although a very valuable one, to ground

photography, and both make little sense unless they are preceded and accompanied by a study of both the conventional written sources and, occasionally, of the oral tradition. Any site needs to be approached with what one might call a multiple perspective, with the senses as well as with the intellect and the ability to digest print.

The present work is not a gazetteer. It is not a comprehensive survey of industrial Britain from the air. One day, no doubt, such a survey will be prepared, but *Industrial History from the Air* is not that book. Its intentions are much more modest, to indicate the various ways in which aerial photographs can illuminate the development of British industry, broadly interpreted, and to point to certain kinds of site where this can be carried out with particular success. There is no preference for eighteenth- and nineteenth-century sites over more modern ones, no suggestion that heavy industry is more worthy of attention than light. It is never implied that every piece of information of value has been squeezed from a photograph. What is assumed throughout is that industrial sites are quite as worthy of study from the air as those relating to Bronze Age archaeology, and as much entitled to space in the photographic archives.

The sections into which the book is divided – Quarrying, Mining, Manufacturing, Industrial Estates, Inland Waterways, Ports and Docks, Railways, Airports and Airfields, New Towns and Model Villages – are deliberately wide. Each of them could easily be subdivided many times, but there seemed to be no special point in doing so, since the aim is to be illustrative, not definitive.

In a number of instances, a site could sensibly and logically be included under more than one heading. What, for example, is one to do about a photograph of a stretch of Bedfordshire which shows both brick-kilns and the pits from which the clay has been dug? A kiln is a species of factory and a clay-pit is a kind of quarry. In which category should the photograph be placed in the book, and how should it be indexed in the archive? Equally, would a photograph of Trafford Park Industrial Estate belong under Manufacturing, since this is the type of activity which is carried on there, or under Inland Waterways, because the site is served by the Manchester Ship Canal? The choice does not really seem to matter, since in every case the most important details relating to each photograph are mentioned both in the accompanying text and in the Index. But it has to be admitted that the method could cause problems for the exceptionally single-minded reader, who is interested solely in, say, brick-kilns or canals, and who has no time at all for manufacturing or quarrying. Someone almost inevitably has to feel disappointed or frustrated.

References

1. Laurent Eynac, *Guide des voyages aériens*, 1924.
2. *Imperial Airways Gazette*, September 1936.

Quarrying

Until the early nineteenth century, most quarrying was on a very small scale, sufficient to meet local demands. Three factors then began to change the situation quite quickly. The first was the growth of the railway network, which made it feasible to transport heavy and bulky loads cheaply over long distances; the second was the demand of the railway constructors for unprecedented quantities of bricks, sand and lime, with which to build tunnels, bridges, viaducts, and stations; and the third was the enormous increase in the population and, linked with it, the creation of large urban communities in areas where there had previously only been green fields. Cities meant bricks, mortar and roofing slates; and city roads, like railway tracks, meant stone and gravel. Railway tracks also meant iron rails, and railway bridges meant cast and wrought iron. The railways stimulated a great rise in the production of iron, much of which came from ore quarried in Britain.

All this amounts to saying that the Industrial Revolution was the direct cause of large holes in the ground, scattered over much of the British Isles in the form of clay pits, limestone quarries, slate quarries, sand and gravel pits and, to a lesser extent, stone quarries. The users of these materials went to a reasonably local source wherever possible, but in some instances, notably that of slate, this was not possible, and where this was the case, the holes in the ground became exceptionally wide and deep, because they were, so to speak, centralised holes. They served the whole country and exported a good deal of their production abroad as well.

There were a few very substantial quarries even in the eighteenth century, before industrialisation and urbanisation really got under way. In Anglesey, for instance, the Parys copper mine supplied much of the nation's requirements of copper and the limestone taken from Portland and the Bath area had markets a long way from the quarries, mainly because both were well placed in the matter of water transport, the first directly by sea and the second by river to Bristol and then by sea to more distant destinations. Portland had direct access to the sea, but in pre-railway days, the journeys undertaken by Bath stone were more complicated. The architect of Brighton Pavilion, for instance, used Bath stone, which would most probably have had to travel down the Avon to Bristol and then, after transhipment to a larger vessel, round Land's End to Brighton. It might conceivably, however, have gone via the Kennet and Avon Canal to Reading and then down the Thames to the sea. In the case of these quarries, exceptional demand made the holes exceptionally big.

From the mid-nineteenth century onwards a series of inventions and technical improvements led to more and even wider and deeper holes in the increasingly ravaged surface of Britain. The Gilchrist–Thomas process (1875) made it possible to use iron ores which had not previously been a practical proposition; the discovery of clays containing a useful proportion of combustible material created the Fletton brick industry and therefore enormous holes over large areas of Bedfordshire and Northamptonshire – a single aerial photograph has the great advantage of showing not one hole, but several, not a single brickworks chimney, but a forest of them; the development of Portland cement necessitated new limestone quarries; reliable cement, available in large quantities, made construction in concrete feasible, and concrete needed sand, gravel and crushed stone as aggregate. The demand for aggregates has increased at a frightening rate during the present century and the consequent pock-marking of the landscape seems to be never-ending.

The most dramatic modifications to the appearance of rural Britain have been caused by the insatiable demand for road-building and road-maintenance materials. Wherever there are easily accessible deposits of suitable granites and hard limestones, the threat of monster quarrying has been present. In some cases, whole hills have been removed in a period of no more than twenty years and views which our parents would have considered practically unchangeable have gone for ever. Previous generations could not have effected destruction on this scale; they did not have the machinery to bring it about or the customers to gobble up the products.

One of the most striking examples of the ability

which modern equipment has to transform the landscape in a relatively short time is to be seen in the china-clay areas of East Cornwall and West Devon. Until the 1940s, the pits were, by present-day standards, tiny. There were a considerable number of them and, mainly because of the complications caused by mineral rights leases, both they and their characteristic moon-surface heaps of waste sand were close together.

The land is now nearly all in the ownership of one company, which has followed the policy of concentrating production on a few very large pits, with correspondingly enormous tips, and of shifting old spoil heaps to provide room for enlarging the pits. The landscape has been noticeably changed as a result.

There is nothing to equal aerial photography as a means of documenting what mineral extraction by means of open pits and quarries has done to change the face of Britain. Many of these sites are difficult to visit and, even when one is able to walk or drive to them, one cannot see them in their spatial context or get a proper idea of their extent. This is especially so where modern planning restrictions have compelled quarry owners to leave the rim of a hill or plateau untouched, so that from even a short distance away on the ground there is nothing of the workings to be seen. Only from above does one realise that the hill now resembles a molar, excavated by the dentist and ready for filling.

What one might term upward dereliction – ugliness, sterility, ruins and waste heaps – has long been considered an unfortunate concomitant of industrialisation and it has been richly recorded by the camera. Downward dereliction, on the other hand, has had to wait for aerial photography in order that its character and extent can be fully appreciated. But it is only fair to point out that not all industrial holes result in dereliction. The National Coal Board has been both scrupulous and imaginative in restoring to agricultural use the sites of modern opencast coal extraction and, apart from certain changes in contour and level, which are usually not obvious, it is not easy to identify the places where such working was in progress only ten years ago. Unfortunately one cannot say the same, at least as yet, about opencast mining for iron ore, where gigantic quarries are unpleasing raw gashes in the countryside; or about limestone quarries, where there appears to be little or no restoration policy. Most gravel workings are in river valleys and fill up quickly with water once extraction has come to an end. The result in some areas is a not unattractive series of man-made lakes, as travellers coming in to land at Heathrow will have noticed.

They are also likely to observe from the same vantage point the huge area of West Middlesex which is now covered by reservoirs, mostly dating from the period since the Second World War, and a token of London's ever-growing suburbs, with their insatiable demand for water, both for industry and for domestic purposes. Victorian England took fewer baths, had no washing machines, and managed with far less water annually for each member of the population. These huge artificial lakes are monuments both to improved hygiene and to gross wastefulness.

The Blue Circle cement works at Westbury, Wiltshire

Portland cement is made from two ingredients, chalk and clay. These are crushed, ground and blended and then heated in a kiln until they fuse together. The cement is discharged from the kiln in the form of nodules, known in the industry as 'clinker'. After this has been cooled, it is ground into the fine grey powder sold as cement.

At Westbury, the chalk – the main raw material – is taken from a quarry about 2.5 km from the works and close to the famous White Horse. Although it is very near the edge of the escarpment with which railway travellers are familiar as their train approaches Westbury station, it cannot be seen at all from the plain on which the works is located. The chalk is taken from the quarry to the works by an underground pipeline which runs about 1.5 m below the surface. Surprisingly, the course of the pipeline cannot be seen in an aerial photograph, even during periods of summer drought.

The works began production in 1962 and, since it requires about 4,000 tonnes of chalk a day and operates continuously, the quarry is now enormous, as aerial photographs show.

The other ingredient, clay, is obtained from pits near the works, on the northern side.

In the siting of the works and the quarries, in the extensive tree-planting programme, and in the measures taken to control dust, the company has achieved environmental standards which are greatly superior to anything the industry knew fifty years ago, when cement manufacturing was synonymous with dirt and pollution.

It is interesting to note that without aerial photographs it is almost impossible to obtain a reasonable impression either of the two sets of quarries or of the layout of the works complex. Even in a drawing, it is necessary to use an aerial perspective in order to show the relation of one building to another.

5 The Blue Circle cement works at Westbury, Wiltshire. Cambridge University Collection, CPO 27: July 1982.

Photograph **5** shows the location and layout of Westbury works as seen from the west. The clay pits can be seen at left centre of the picture. The large clinker-store is the first building on the left, by the edge of the clay-pits, and adjoining this, moving upwards, are the slurry-mixing and storage tanks. The double-gabled building to the right of the clinker store accommodates the clinker-grinding mill; the two long buildings above it and to the right contain the two kilns. The concrete towers between the kilns and the clinker-grinding mill are the silos, from which cement can be loaded into either road or rail tankers. Behind the 120-metre chimney are the buildings of the pulverised refuse plant, which convert 80,000 tonnes of domestic refuse a year into fuel for the kilns. The photograph shows how the prevailing westerly wind carries smoke from the works clear of the town of Westbury, which is situated to the south-west of the picture.

The Exeter–London main railway line is on the right and between this and the works access road are the sidings serving the works. Cement tanker-wagons can be seen on the sidings.

The buildings on the extreme right edge of the picture are those of the Blue Circle social club.

6 The Blue Circle cement works: chalk quarry. Cambridge University Collection, CPO 32: July 1982.

Photograph **6** shows the chalk quarry on the hills which form the northern edge of Salisbury Plain. The crushing plant is slightly to the left of centre and the slurry-pumping plant is close to the right-hand edge of the quarry. The pipeline runs more or less straight from here to a point just to the left of the chimney, burrowing under the railway in order to reach the storage tanks.

The Bedfordshire brickfield

'Bedfordshire brickfield' is a convenient shorthand term for the huge brickmaking region which extends into Cambridgeshire, north Buckinghamshire and Northamptonshire, although the major part of it is, in fact, in Bedfordshire. Geologically, it is the Oxford Clay area. It was of little industrial importance until the end of the nineteenth century, when it was discovered that the shale-like clay, containing about twenty per cent of moisture, could be pressed into a brick which could be fired immediately, without any previous drying. An equally important advantage was that the composition of this clay includes something like ten per cent of carbonaceous material, which burns during the firing process and reduces the amount of fuel required to roughly a third of what is required when other clays are used.

The new method of brickmaking, which was highly mechanised from the beginning, was pioneered at Fletton, south of Peterborough, and was soon adopted by other firms within the same clay area. The Forder Company's works at Pillinge – now known as Stewartby – in Bedfordshire was producing what were then known as Flettons in 1897.

During the 1920s many of the smaller firms ran into financial difficulties and three large companies, the Marston Valley Brick Company, Redland, and the London Brick Company, came into being as a result of mergers and take-overs. These now produce, at their various works, not all of them in this part of the country, more than half of all the bricks used in Britain. The London Brick

7 **Brickworks at Stewartby, Bedfordshire.** Cambridge University Collection, CPP 2: January 1982.

Company is the largest brickmaker in the world.

Until the 1930s only what is known in the trade as a common brick was produced in the area. This was the brick mainly used for the great expansion of London during the first forty years of the present century. Subsequently, however, large quantities of facing bricks were made here too. Despite high transport costs, the scale of production and thoroughgoing mechanisation made it possible for Flettons to compete successfully over most of Britain with bricks made in local yards. It was this, more than any other factor, which caused so many small brickworks to close down during the 1920s and 1930s and again, in a second wave of casualties, during the 1940s and 1950s.

The Bedfordshire brickfield is mainly flat and treeless and the chimneys of the brickworks dominate the landscape. The trend is towards taller chimneys – those of 90 m are common here – as the most effective way of dealing with the serious pollution problems, which are a constant worry both to the local planning and health authorities, and to the companies themselves.

The waste gases from the kilns contain fluorine compounds and sulphur oxides, which kill trees and are dangerous to farm livestock.

The brick industry has changed the landscape in another way; its enormous clay-pits and waste dumps have made thousands of acres of once fertile land derelict. This problem, however, is gradually finding a partial solution. Some of the pits are being filled with household refuse from the London area, brought in by rail, and others are being tidied up and made suitable for various water sports.

Photograph **7** shows Stewartby works, southeast of Bedford, and, nearby, Stewartby village. B. J. H. Forder started his brickworks in 1897 at what was then known as Wootton Pillinge, a hamlet of twelve cottages. The works, which subsequently passed under the control of the London Brick Company, is now the largest brick-producing unit in the world. Stewartby village owes its existence entirely to the brick industry, although many of the people who live there now work elsewhere. Like the works, it was named after the then Chairman of the Company, Sir Malcolm

11

8 Brickfield panorama around Orton Longueville, Cambridgeshire. Cambridge University Collection, BIR 91: June 1972.

Stewart, and a former Chairman, Sir Harley Stewart. The first houses were built in 1926 and there is now a population of about 1,000, living in 358 houses and bungalows.

When it was established, Stewartby was well served by the railway from Oxford to Cambridge, which crossed the site and made convenient connections with five north–south main lines. Now only the Bletchley–Bedford section survives. Part of it can be seen running from the left centre of the picture towards the chimneys of the works. Stewartby village lies towards the top left-hand corner, located so as to be usually well clear of the fumes from the chimneys.

The adjacent clay-pit occupies most of the centre of the photograph. In order to reach the beds of Lower Oxford Clay, which are used for brickmaking, the top layer of soil and clay has to be stripped off, and this can be seen lying in piles along the bottom of the pit which has already been worked.

Photograph **8** taken ten years earlier than **7**, gives an excellent impression of the treeless brickfield panorama around Orton Longueville, in Cambridgeshire, south-west of Peterborough. The ravaged landscape here is all too apparent, with the tipped ridges of over-burden making the worked-out pits look not unlike a giant's potatofields.

The big circular reservoir at top centre of the picture serves a group of brickworks, as well as the residential area to the north-east. The depth to which the clay is excavated is well illustrated by the pit-edge at left centre, below the works, where the division between the bottom layer of brickmaking clay and the almost equally thick top layer of unwanted soil is clearly visible.

Limestone quarries at Portland, Dorset

The quarries on Portland were worked for local use during the whole of the medieval period, and

9 **Limestone quarries, Portland, Dorset.** Cambridge University Collection, AMN 74: December 1965.

by the beginning of the fourteenth century Portland stone was being exported in considerable quantities. It went to Exeter, for work on the cathedral, to Christ Church, Oxford, and, above all, to London, where it was used in the construction of the Royal Palace and King's Chapel at Westminster, and in the Tower of London. The location of the quarries made it possible to load the stone directly into sea-going ships, a commercial advantage which was exploited to the full during the following centuries.

The quarries fell on hard times during the fifteenth century, but a boom period set in early in the seventeenth, when Portland stone became very fashionable, especially in London. The rapidly increasing demand during the second half of the seventeenth century, partly as a result of the need to rebuild much of London after the Great Fire, resulted in a larger-scale and more efficient organisation of the quarries, and prices fell rapidly.

Portland's excellent weathering qualities make it a particularly suitable stone for the exterior of city buildings. Throughout the seventeenth, eighteenth and nineteenth centuries, it was a scarce commodity and there was great competition to obtain it. The beds most suitable for external use lie at a considerable depth, and up to 12 m of soil, rubble and stone have to be removed in order to reach them. The waste tips are consequently extensive and, seen from the air, much of Portland presents a very dug-over appearance. It would, in fact, be no great exaggeration to describe the island as one vast stone quarry.

Until the railway reached Portland in 1865, all the stone shipped from the island was loaded from wooden piers along the east coast. It was taken from the quarry to the ship balanced on two-wheeled waggons, pulled by eight or ten horses. The first crane arrived in Portland in 1853 and before that the skill and effort required to manhandle blocks weighing as much as 10 tonnes almost defeats the imagination.

Quarrying at Portland nowadays is on a greatly

10 **Limestone quarries, Portland, Dorset.** Cambridge University Collection, AS 14: June 1948.

reduced scale and most of the old quarry workings have been abandoned for many years.

Photograph **9** was taken from the south, looking towards the Dorset coast. The south-east breakwater sheltering one side of the naval base can be seen at the top left-hand corner, with a number of the buildings belonging to the base just south of it. Moving along this coast of the island, one notices HM Prison towards the right of the picture. The prison playing fields, slightly inland and to the left of the prison, were laid out on the levelled surface of an old quarry.

The steepness of the cliffs on the left is obvious and shows clearly why it was necessary to haul stone across the island to the piers on the other and gentler side. Rows of back-to-back quarrymen's cottages are in the centre of the photograph, most of the other housing being more recent. The workshops of the Bath and Portland Stone Company, which today has a monopoly of quarry-working on Portland, are in the centre of the right-hand edge of the picture.

Photograph **10** is an earlier picture. It allows

one to see the mixture of farming and quarrying which is characteristic of Portland and indicates very well how the quarrymen were continuously nibbling forward into the surrounding agricultural land from the area which had already been dealt with. The different beds of stone can be easily distinguished on the photograph. The aerial photography makes it possible to understand what an enormously time- and energy-consuming task stone-quarrying on Portland was. So much nuisance-stone had to be removed and tipped, by the most laborious hand methods, in order to reach and extract the layers which were the point and purpose of the industry.

One needs a photograph like this in order to remind oneself of the scale and difficulty of the quarrymen's task, before they had machinery to help them. In 1812, 800 men and boys, 180 horses and 50 ships were engaged in the stone trade of Portland, which was probably about double the number employed a century earlier. The 800 men produced, hauled and loaded about 25,000 tonnes of saleable stone each year, or roughly 30 tonnes a

14

11 Hamdon Hill quarries, Somerset. Cambridge University Collection, ARE 24: May 1967.

head. To do this, they had to shift perhaps 100,000 tonnes of over-burden of one kind and another, say a further 100 tonnes a head. A picture of this kind increases one's admiration for this achievement.

Hamdon Hill quarries, Somerset

At Hamdon Hill, more usually known nowadays as Ham Hill, near Yeovil, the distinctive tawny-coloured stone has been worked since Roman times. The best quality stone, as used in the building of Montacute House, is durable and can be easily dressed to fine limits, but what remains of the beds containing this grade of stone is now at a depth which is uneconomic to work, even with the help of modern machinery.

The lower grades are fairly close to the surface and they are virtually the only ones to be used today, not as quarried blocks, but in the form of what is called reconstituted stone, that is, a con-crete using the crushed stone as an aggregate. The biggest customer for reconstituted Ham Hill stone is a concrete products firm in nearby Ilminster.

The quarries on Ham Hill are now owned, like those on Portland, by the Bath and Portland Stone Group.

On the occasion when photograph **11** was taken, the main interest was not the quarries, but the Iron Age hill fort which at one time occupied the hill. The fact that the collection at Cambridge contains an excellent photograph of the Hamdon Hill quarries is an accident, for which one should be grateful. The ditch and bank surrounding the fort are very clear in the picture.

The village of East Stoke is to be seen in the top right corner. Stoke-sub-Hamdon is just out of the picture, beyond the top left corner. The present workings are those at the top end of the hill and the road to them has been improved sufficiently to allow modern lorries to reach the quarry. There are a few cottages on the hill itself,

15

12 Torr Quarry, near East Cranmore, Somerset. Cambridge University Collection, CPT 45: July 1982.

especially at the bottom right corner, but most of the quarrymen lived in one or other of the nearby villages.

The stone quarries of East Mendip

Stone has been quarried all along Mendip for centuries, but until the 1960s extraction was on a small scale and made little change to the appearance of the landscape. Since the Second World War, and especially since the early 1960s, the situation has become entirely different. With the enormous increase in the demand for stone for building and resurfacing roads, it became practicable to think of much bigger production units. Two of these in particular operate on such a scale that within half a century large stretches of Mendip will have simply ceased to exist. The size of what has been accomplished so far can only be fully appreciated from the air.

What is being blasted out of Mendip is a carboniferous limestone of exceptionally high quality. It is dry, consistent in density, and has a high

impact resistance, making it particularly suitable for road-making.

The Torr Quarry

Torr Quarry, near East Cranmore, shown in photograph 12, is now the largest quarrying unit in Britain. It has an interesting history. In 1923, Foster Yeoman, at that time manager of an iron and steel works in the North of England, decided to move south. He rented 60 ha of land at Dulcote, Somerset, in an area which had produced the stone for Wells Cathedral, took on 150 unemployed men and opened a quarry, mainly to supply road-making materials. The business developed very little between the Wars and by the 1950s Foster Yeoman decided that the quarry was in the wrong place. He bought a large site at East Cranmore and began operations there in 1964, and soon afterwards built a 1.5-km rail link to the old Cheddar Valley branch line, which allowed him to move stone by rail to the junction at Witham Friary, and from there by Western Region's main-line system. Once this had been done, he was in a position to transport complete

16

13 **Whatley Quarry, west of Frome, Somerset.** Cambridge University Collection, BKB 35: July 1972.

train-loads of stone to depots in the South-East, which is the most rewarding market. Twenty per cent of Torr's production leaves the works by road, mostly as coated material for surfacing.

Torr Quarry produces about four million tonnes of stone a year and it is expected to have a life of 50 years, when it will have been worked downwards to a depth of about 100 m. At the end of its career as a working quarry, it could well become a reservoir, large enough for boating and other aquatic activities on a considerable scale.

The photograph shows three other quarries in addition to Torr. The smallest of them would have been considered large in the 1930s. When the photograph was taken Torr Quarry was being worked to a depth of 60 m. In twenty years' time, a large part of the area will have been excavated down to getting on for twice that depth. It will be a prodigious hole, somewhat deep for a boating lake, one might think.

The crushing plant and storage bins are in the centre of the picture. The railway line goes under the main road, and its route is plainly visible. Nearly 5,000 trains a year travel along it.

Whatley Quarry

Whatley Quarry, south of Mells and west of Frome, has been operating since the mid-1930s. It now belongs to the Amey Roadstone Corporation. From an annual production of 225,000 tonnes in 1936, the quarry now has a capacity of about three million tonnes a year, but is at present producing about two-thirds of that.

The railway facilities here were installed in 1964. Here, as at Torr, it was possible, with the help of a short spur line, to make use of an existing line, the one between Radstock and Frome, which had been used mainly to transport coal from the colliery at Radstock.

Photograph **13** is possibly more spectacular than that of Torr, mainly because the hillside is somewhat steeper and the system of extraction rather different, in order to meet the special demands of the site. The crushing plant is in the

17

14 Delabole slate quarry, St Teath, Cornwall. Cambridge University Collection, AOP 40: June 1966.

centre of the picture, to the left of the conical pile, and in front of it is the storage building, from which stone is discharged straight into waiting trains. The coating plant is in the left foreground.

Part of another quarry, not belonging to the same company, is seen in the top corner of the picture.

Delabole slate quarry, Cornwall

Delabole slate quarry, in the parish of St Teath, has been in production for nearly 600 years, an exceptionally long life for any quarry. It was considerably enlarged between 1750 and 1800 and continued to prosper throughout the nineteenth century. By 1882 it was 395 m long and 120 m deep and was producing 1,000 tonnes of finished slate a day. In 1937 the quarry had reached a depth of 140 m and its circumference was about 1.5 km. At that time it was employing 350 people. It is still in production, although on a greatly reduced scale.

Delabole slate has been used for many purposes. Large quantities of excellent roofing slates came from here and slabs were also sold for kitchen floors, window-sills, corn chests, vats, mantelpieces and water cisterns. Few roofing slates are made today and the quarry survives by selling slate powder for the plastics, cosmetics and paint industries, slate granules for surfacing concrete roofing tiles, and building and walling stone.

The rail link between Delabole and Wade-bridge was closed in 1967, and everything the quarry produces now has to go by road.

Photograph **14** was taken in 1966, the year before the railway was shut down. The line curves round the top half of the photograph, with the station serving Delabole village near the top left edge, and the quarry siding branching off it before the line reaches the village of Pengelly, on the extreme left. The quarry workshops cover a large part of the centre of the picture.

A notable feature of Delabole quarry has always been the high proportion of waste. In 1937 it pro-

15 Great Oakley slate quarry, Gwynedd. Cambridge University Collection, AET 77: May 1962.

duced 10,000 tonnes of slate and 250,000 of waste. Over the centuries the waste has been nearly all tipped in the area shown in the lower half of the photograph, a practice which has resulted in a huge artificial plateau, a large part of which now accommodates the workshops.

The labour force never exceeded 600, and until 1855 it included a number of women and girls. There would therefore have been no difficulty in housing them at a fairly short walking distance from their work, either in Delabole or Pengelly, or in other settlements within the 2,400 ha parish of St Teath. St Teath itself is 5 km to the south of the quarry.

Great Oakley slate quarry, Gwynedd

There is evidence that Welsh slate has been used for roofing since Roman times, but an organised industry dates only from the second half of the eighteenth century, when a considerable increase in house-building created a market which was interesting to men with capital to invest. From

then until the outbreak of the Second World War in 1939, the North Wales slate industry did reasonably well, although with considerable fluctuations in trade. Since then, the story has been a dismal one. Quarry after quarry closed down, some as a result of mismanagement, but many more in the face of competition from mass-produced concrete, asbestos tiles and foreign slate. Another, and less publicised reason for the decline, was the shortage of suitable labour. It was a dangerous and poorly paid industry, and few men were willing to continue in it if they could find an alternative.

Great Oakley quarry, one mile north-west of Blaenau Ffestiniog, is shown in **15**. The slate formation in most of this area dips deeply under the mountains, so that the slate has usually been mined, not quarried. At the Oakley quarry, the chambers were as large as 36 m long, 12 m wide and 30 m high. The miners reached them by means of zigzag staircases made of slabs of waste slate.

The quarry dates from 1755. The Oakley family

19

16 China-clay panorama near St Stephen-in-Brannel, Cornwall. Cambridge University Collection, BMB 102: March 1973.

were considerable landowners and quarry operators in the area and by the mid-nineteenth century the Oakley quarry was one of the largest and most successful in the Ffestiniog district. Early in the present century there were 80 kilometres of railways in the mines and the underground workings extended to a depth of more than 400 m. There were twelve slate mills, all worked by electricity.

The quarry closed in 1971, but has subsequently reopened, on a very reduced scale.

The aerial photograph gives a good impression of how the Oakley quarry operated. Each mine, a gallery driven into the side of the mountain, had its own waste tip and its own mill, where the blocks of slate taken out of the mine were cut and split. Eight of the twelve mills in use at Oakley can be seen in the photograph.

The finished slate was taken to the bottom of the mountain by a system of steep, cable-controlled light railways. The system had a number of focal points, one of which can be seen, together with a

group of quarrymen's cottages, at the bottom left-hand corner of the picture. Slate extraction and processing on this scale and with this amount of mechanisation obviously demanded a great deal of capital. The companies which were unable to afford it were usually the first to disappear.

China-clay panorama near St Stephen-in-Brannel, Cornwall

The granite found in Devon and Cornwall is usually whitish and composed of quartz, felspar and mica. The decomposition of the felspar, by a process known as kaolinisation, produces china-clay. More than ninety per cent of the china-clay so far produced in Britain has come from the granite massif of Henbarrow, to the north and west of St Austell, but the Lee Moor area, on the south-west slopes of Dartmoor, above Plymouth, is increasingly important.

Over much of the Cornish moorland, china-

20

clay could at one time be found very close to the surface. In the mid-eighteenth century, the time of Cookworthy, Wedgwood and Spode, the pits were very small and little trouble and expense were needed to open them. Most of the clay beds worked today, however, lie under layers of earth and rock which may be as much as 9 m thick. Even in the best pits, substantial quantities of stone and undecomposed granite have to be removed. This is a process which until thirty years ago demanded a great deal of hand labour.

In recent years, clay workings have been taken to a depth of more than 120 m, but the bottom of the deposit has never yet been reached. Extraction to greater depths is possible, but demands considerable widening of the pit and, with the area so congested with old pits and old waste-tips, this is very difficult to achieve.

The organisation and techniques of the industry today bear little relation to what was done before the Second World War. Mechanisation of extraction and scientific control of processing have revolutionised production, but the fundamental problem remains – ninety per cent of what is removed from the pits has to be dumped as unprofitable waste, clean sand and mica. Although an increasing proportion of this finds some commercial use nowadays, mostly as building aggregates, the white hills which characterise the landscape of the china-clay districts continue to grow bigger.

Photograph **16** shows part of the western end of Henbarrow. The large pit in the foreground is Goonvean, where production began at the end of the eighteenth century, and at left centre is Trethosa. Above and to the left of Trethosa is Kernick and at top right is Treviscoe. These pits are all operational, but dotted over the landscape in between them one can distinguish the sites of numerous small pits, which have not been worked for many years.

Goonvean illustrates the modern method of removing the clay. High-pressure water-jets, positioned on the terraces, are directed against the quarry face. A slurry containing the china-clay is washed down to the bottom of the pit, from where it is pumped to the settling tanks, on the left of the pit. Here the mica, sand and other waste material is removed, and the clay-slurry is taken to a drying plant. Each pit has its own batch of settling tanks, but nowadays the clay-slurry is piped to a drying plant serving a group of pits. The drying plant for this particular group is at upper right centre of the picture.

The rock and sand waste from the pit are taken straight to the tip as work progresses. The Goonvean tip is outside the photograph to the right, but those for Trethosa and Kernick can be clearly seen.

China-clay extraction uses a great deal of water. The pipeline supplying Goonvean runs along the edge of the pit, just behind the houses. A system of collection and filtration allows a high proportion of the water to be recycled.

In the British Isles mining, in the precise sense of the word – it is often used loosely to include quarrying – means mainly coal-mining, although underground working has also been employed to extract metallic ores, especially lead, and, in one or two areas, stone. Because it takes place below the surface, mining might appear, at first sight, to be a singularly unpromising subject for aerial photography, but this is not in fact so, because although the actual winning of the coal or ore may take place many metres underground and its history therefore remains invisible from above, the equally important activities at ground level often leave many interesting clues behind them, which remain for many years, sometimes for centuries, after a mine has closed, and these are particularly clear and significant when viewed from the air.

It is impossible for mining to proceed without disturbing the surface of the ground in some way. The most obvious and spectacular instances of this are the tips, often of great size, on which the stone and other unsaleable products from the mining operation have been deposited. One does not, of course, need aerial photography to see these, but where the God's-eye view can be of immense help is in plotting and comprehending the pattern of these tips, especially when the mines to which they were once linked are no longer functioning and all the surface installations have been cleared away. In general, small tips mean small pits, and the smaller the tip, the earlier the pit was worked out and eventually closed down. But a pit is not necessarily the same as a colliery. Some collieries extracted coal from two or more pits in the course of their working life and, if one has taken the precaution of informing oneself about the history of the colliery and the area beforehand, the grouping of the waste-heaps into a single mining unit becomes clear from an aerial photograph.

The disappearance of a colliery or even the abandoning of a whole coalfield does not mean the obliteration of all traces of a former mining community, however. In most cases, the houses where the miners used to live and the churches, pubs, shops and other buildings of what was once a logically situated settlement still exist. The advantage of recording and studying them by means of a photograph taken from the air is that one can observe the shape and pattern of the community and see how its buildings related to the roads and railways which served the colliery and to the site of the colliery itself. One can also see how oppressively and dangerously close, in many cases, the waste tips came to the houses.

This kind of thinking relates, of course, to the local coal-mining methods of the nineteenth and twentieth centuries. For earlier periods, the surviving evidence is quite different and much of it is intelligible only from the air. In the North-East and parts of the Midlands, coal was mined during the sixteenth and seventeenth centuries and, in places, into the eighteenth, by sinking a shaft, often no more than 6 m deep, until the seam had been reached and then extending the bottom of the shaft outwards for as far as was judged safe. The soil and rock were hauled to the surface by means of a rope and windlass and dumped around the edges of the pit. The coal followed by the same route. When the limits of safety had been reached in one of these bell-shaped pits, it was abandoned and another started a short distance away. After fifty or a hundred years of producing coal this way, a large area would be covered with little bun-shaped mounds, which make impressive aerial photographs. In no other way can one appreciate the Toytown scale of mining of these two- and three-man enterprises before the days of steam-power for pumping and haulage, when the industrial demand for coal was very small and when, as a domestic fuel, coal was used only by those who could not afford wood.

The same bell-pit technique was used for extracting metallic ores, especially lead, but less frequently. The more usual evidence of metal-mining, as seen from the air, consists of an obviously disturbed area of countryside, with the waste material left in what now appear to be haphazard heaps and ridges. There is much of this to be seen on Mendip, where lead-mining was carried out in both Roman and medieval times, and in West Cornwall, where generations of tin-mining have produced a land surface which looks as if it had been very roughly cultivated with a giant spade.

17 Coal mines at Catherton Common, Shropshire. Cambridge University Collection, CIJ 74: February 1979.

Coal mines at Catherton Common, Shropshire

Catherton Common is close to the village of Farlow, 5 km north-west of Cleobury Mortimer. On the slopes of Clee Hill, much of the land offers little possibility for farming of any kind, and during the later medieval period parts of it were used for mining coal. With the equipment and techniques of the time this was possible only where the seams were very close to the surface. Photograph **17** shows the results of such primitive mining. The method, to dig a pick-and-shovel hole 2.0–2.5 m deep, broadened out at the bottom as far as was safe for the man working inside it, and then to take out as much coal as one could before the hole showed signs of falling in, is so obvious and, within broad limits, so independent of period, that workings of this kind cannot, in the absence of any written record, be dated with anything approaching certainty. They are just as likely to be early sixteenth-century as late thirteenth.

What is perhaps more interesting than to attempt to date the pits is to try to recreate the culture and technology of the people responsible for them. The miners were probably families who lived in rough huts on this heath land and earned some sort of living by digging out the coal. Each pit required only two people working on it, one to dig and the other to haul up the coal. It was a very suitable job for a family, with the man doing the heavy work extracting the coal and his wife or older children looking after the haulage. When they had got all they could from one pit, they simply started another. How many families were involved at any given time and how long it took them to exhaust a pit, it is impossible to say, although it would not be too difficult to arrange an experiment in order to find out and it is curious that so far this has never been done.

The quantities involved were very small, although it is evident from the waste-heaps surrounding them that some pits must have been bigger than others. One could surmise, however,

23

18 Iron mines at Bentley Grange, Emley, South Yorkshire. Cambridge University Collection, GU 37: July 1951.

that very few of these pits would have yielded more than a ton of coal and some a good deal less. A major and unsolved problem is to decide what happened to the coal once it had reached the surface. The probability is that it was transported by pack-horse to blacksmiths and possibly to potters as well, working within a fairly small distance from Catherton Common, but one cannot be certain about this.

It will be noticed that several pits, especially on the left-hand side of the picture, have fallen in completely, and one wonders why this did not happen more generally. It may possibly have something to do with the geological formation or with the foolhardiness of the miners, who took out more coal than was really safe.

Iron mines at Bentley Grange, Emley, South Yorkshire

The technique illustrated at Catherton Common was not peculiar to coal-mining. From the twelfth century until the sixteenth, iron ore was extracted in this way at a number of sites, including Bentley Grange, 10 km to the north-west of Barnsley. The spoil-heaps here are large and widely spaced, and as much as 2 m high, as one sees in **18**. These suggest a pit of between 4.5 and 7.5 m deep, with galleries radiating as much as 3 m from it. The curious tam-o-shanter effect is the result of the shaft subsiding and trees and bushes establishing themselves in the depression produced.

Bentley Grange was an outlying property of the

24

19 Lead mines near Forest, Co. Durham. Cambridge University Collection, BEW 2: February 1971.

Cistercian foundation, Byland Abbey, which was 74 km away. The Abbey had a forge 5 km from the iron ore deposits, at Denby, and the ore was smelted there. The charcoal for the Denby furnaces also came from Bentley.

Bentley does not seem to have been an iron-mining settlement. There is no evidence that a village ever existed there. However, the buildings shown in the bottom right-hand corner of the photograph are those of the farm known as Bentley Grange. They contain masonry which pre-dates the dissolution of the monasteries and it is possible that there were monastic farm-buildings here, which included accommodation for the iron-miners. The iron ore would, in any case, have had to be stored somewhere, while waiting to be transported to Denby and the grange, or a site very close to it, seems the logical place for this, especially since the horses used for haulage would have required to be fed and watered somewhere.

Lead mines near Forest, Co. Durham

The early method of working lead ore was to dig pits 4.5–6.0 m deep, strung out along the outcropping veins of ore. From the sides of these pits, probably during the seventeenth century, the miners followed the narrow strings of ore until the vein became too narrow to work in. Subsidence was usually not the main problem in lead-mining, since the pits and galleries were cut through hard rock, but the ventilation of these small workings became poor as the workings advanced beyond the bottom of the shaft, so each pit was soon abandoned and another one started further along the vein.

Photograph 19 shows this very well. One can easily follow the course of the veins on it, one going north and the other east and west. Because the excavated debris was mostly rock, the pits have not fallen in to the same extent as in early

25

20 Old coal pits at Garforth, West Yorkshire. Cambridge University Collection, BMF 10: April 1973.

coal-mining and the outline of the circular shafts is still sharp and clear.

Old coal pits at Garforth, West Yorkshire

Coal has been mined at Garforth since the eighteenth century, although the area is less important nowadays, and the principal modern workings are to be found further east, in the direction of Selby.

Photograph **20** is exceptionally interesting, because it documents coal-mining at Garforth over a long period. In the bottom half of the picture, west of the road, one can see, as soil-marks, the traces of a number of early pits. The surface of the ground has been completely levelled and consolidated and has been returned to agriculture. The closeness of the pits, however, indicates that they were shallow and operated before the

introduction of steam-pumps, which made it possible to keep deeper pits free from water.

The colliery above the road is nineteenth-century and was still operating in 1973, when the picture was taken. The modern pit can be seen at top centre, with its railway sidings running down towards the road that crosses the picture diagonally. The waste-tips of the modern pit occupy a large part of the centre of the photograph.

Mining subsidence near Little Addington, Northamptonshire

The mining here was for limestone and the spacing of the holes caused by the mine collapsing suggests that pillars of stone were left to support the roof as work proceeded. Photograph **21** was taken in November 1974, but one could have guessed the time of the year to within a week or two from what is to be seen in the surrounding

21 Mining subsidence near Little Addington, Northamptonshire. Cambridge University Collection, BRT 84: November 1974.

fields, three of which have been ploughed before winter sets in, while two more are still covered by the straw left after the corn was combined.

The subsidence would appear to have occurred not long before the corn crop on the field would have been harvested, possibly in June.

The depth of topsoil can be clearly seen from an examination of the rim of one or two of the larger holes. The restoration of the field to agriculture would have been a difficult process, even if it had been thought to be worth attempting.

Chatterley Whitfield colliery, Tunstall, Staffordshire

The North Staffordshire coalfield covers a triangular area of about 310 square kilometres, with the city of Stoke-on-Trent at its approximate centre. Chatterley Whitfield colliery lies in the north-east of the coalfield, close to the surface outcrops of the coal seams. There are late thirteenth-century references to mining in the manor of Tunstall and outcrop working on a small scale continued until the eighteenth century. Deeper pits, using steam-driven pumps and winding-gear, were operating during the first half of the nineteenth century and further shafts were being sunk up to 1917.

In 1974, it was decided that Chatterley Whitfield coal could be more easily worked from the nearby Wolstanton colliery and an underground roadway was driven to connect the two pits. In 1976 the surface installations at Chatterley Whitfield came to the end of their life and two years later a Trust was set up to establish a museum of coal-mining on the site.

27

22 Chatterley Whitfield colliery, Tunstall, Staffordshire. Archive of National Smokeless Fuels Ltd.: 1960.

The two photographs, **22**, dating from 1960, when the colliery was still operating, and the other **23**, taken twenty-two years later, show the results of closure and gradual rehabilitation of the area. Photograph **22** was taken from the air, **23** from the top of a reclaimed spoil-tip which, reshaped and sown to grass, is now only one-third of its original height.

The major difference between the appearance of the site as it was up to 1976 and as it is today is the cleaning up and landscaping of the spoil-heaps and dumps of all kinds which used to surround the workings. The removal of much of the conveyor system leading to the spoil-heaps and of the railway tracks which ran through the pithead installations has also helped to give the whole area an archaeological, rather than an industrial look.

The various buildings shown on **23** (nearly, but not quite, as clearly as they would have appeared in an aerial photograph) are as follows. Beginning at the extreme left of the photograph, the twin-gabled building used to be the colliery warehouse. The curiously-shaped building in front of it, with four arches in its façade, is at the top of the Winstanley shaft. Completed in 1914, and named after the Company's mining engineer, Robert Winstanley, this was sunk for ventilation purposes only and was never used to wind coal.

In front of the Winstanley building and running off to the right is what remains of the railway cutting, which was constructed in 1878 to take coal to the lower Tunstall branch of the North Staffordshire Railway. The colliery's main boiler house (1938) is the long building at the back of the chimney, with the old power station running at right angles to it towards the railway cutting.

To the right of the chimney is the Institute shaft (1874), and beyond that the Platt shaft (1883). The Institute was so named to commemorate the visit of the North Staffordshire Institute of Mining Engineers to the colliery. Previously it had been called the Bellringer. The fourth shaft to be seen in the photograph, at the

23 Chatterley Whitfield colliery: closure and rehabilitation. Archive of National Smokeless Fuels Ltd.: 1982.

extreme right, is that of the Hesketh pit, completed in 1917 and named after Col. George Hesketh, who was Chairman of the colliery company. It was taken to a depth of nearly 600 m. The Hesketh winding-house is to the left of the shaft. It contains a horizontal steam-engine, with 36-inch cylinders and a 72-inch stroke. The power-house is the slightly lower building to the left of the winding-house and continuous with it.

The main repair shops are the long building behind the Institute shaft and at right angles to the Hesketh winding house. The modern buildings at the back of the mine complex and including the square brick tower contain the new pithead baths and canteen (1938) and the office block (1934). The colliery's first canteen facilities were provided by an ex-army hut, in 1920.

The working system in Chatterley Whitfield's latter days is well shown in the 1960 aerial view, **22**. The coal was brought up the Hesketh shaft, the pithead gear of which can be seen in the centre of the picture, and taken by conveyor through the right-angled group of buildings, with light-coloured roofs. Here it was cleaned and sorted and the waste moved along the long covered conveyor extending from the buildings to the extreme left-hand edge of the photograph. At this point it was transferred to an open conveyor, for its final journey up to the tip. The coal was discharged from the right-hand side of the long white building into railway trucks waiting below.

The smaller building with a white roof, to the left of the sorting building in **22** was the mine-car repair shop.

An abandoned coal mine at Dalmellington, Strathclyde

Dalmellington colliery has been closed for many years. The abandoned workings, and the waste-tips associated with them, can be seen in the top left-hand corner of photograph **24**. The purpose of including this photograph here, however, is to illustrate what happens to a community when the main source of its livelihood is taken away.

29

24 Abandoned coal mine at Dalmellington, Strathclyde. Cambridge University Collection, BGZ 81: July 1971.

The area in the centre of the picture was occupied until the 1960s by an estate of semi-detached houses similar to those shown in the bottom right-hand corner. Once the mine had closed, there was no possibility of finding work for so many people in the immediate area, although alternative employment was available within reasonable daily travelling distance for a proportion of them. A large part of Dalmellington's housing stock was therefore demolished. The oval road pattern shows where it used to be, a sadly wasted capital investment.

Dalmellington employed a considerable number of people for many years, a fact which is attested by the size of the cemetery, middle right. The photograph also provides interesting evidence of one of the more significant social revolutions which have occurred since the Second World War. Today's mining families, almost without exception, possess motor cars. The surviving part of the estate at Dalmellington has, it will be observed, no garages. Parking for such cars as did

exist here when the photograph was taken had to be either in the street or in the passages by the side of the houses.

Tin-mining sites near St Hilary, Cornwall

The principal tin-mining areas of Cornwall are to be found west of Truro, the most important being around St Just-in-Penwith, where tin was being mined in the seventeenth century and is still being mined today. One lode runs east from Newlyn and under the sea to Marazion and Porthleven and another, along the north coast, from Pendeen to St Ives. In all these areas, there are dozens of ruined chimneys and engine-houses as monuments to nineteenth-century mining.

A great deal of smaller-scale tin-mining was carried on, however, long before the days of deep mines and steam pumping-engines. One area where there is a great deal of evidence of this is

25 Tin-mining sites near St Hilary, Cornwall. Cambridge University Collection, AOP 92: June 1966.

along the first part of the B 3280 road, after it has branched off the A 394 just east of Marazion (photograph **25**). The pits are within a very small belt of land, showing how narrow the tin-bearing lode was and how closely it was followed. The spoil-heaps, it will be noticed, are large, their size being a consequence of the hard rock below. The tin-miners had to cut their way through granite, an extremely arduous task, given the tools available in the sixteenth and seventeenth centuries, when these pits were dug and worked. With little or no danger of the roof falling in, the only problem was that of ventilation and the miners worked as far along and across the lode as they could from

each shaft. Given this method of proceeding, the ten or so pits to be seen in the picture would have been sufficient to exhaust completely the possibilities of the 800 m or so of tin-bearing lode within the area covered by this picture, a process taking perhaps two hundred years.

In the eighteenth century, tin-smelters are known to have existed at St Erth and at Ludgvan. Both of these places are about 10 km from St Hilary and taking the ore to the smelter, probably by pack-horse, must have been no small venture. The road running between the pits dates from mining days. It was an indispensable part of the operation of the mines.

Manufacturing

A few factories were planned and built as a single, tidy unit and have stayed like that ever since, but they are rare. Processes change and firms grow, and most industrial premises have to adapt themselves to new conditions. Aerial photographs allow us to see exactly what has happened, in a way that nothing else can. They make it possible for us to see how an industrial plant has changed over the years.

A car factory is a perfect illustration of this. At Cowley, for example, William Morris took over the buildings of a former military academy just before the First World War, and adapted them to car assembly. From then on, there were additions to the plant almost every year, further land being bought as required, and the works now covers an area of more than 120 ha. But very little has ever been demolished and the original military academy is still there and in use as an administrative block, so that what one has today is a large complex of buildings which, properly interpreted, tells the story of the company. When one walks around it, one has no feeling whatever of orderly growth. The impression is simply that of an *ad hoc* accretion of buildings and there are few easier places in which to get lost. But from the air the bits begin to fit together, and one can see a pattern emerging. One can also see the relation of the factory to the railway sidings which have served it for getting on for three-quarters of a century and to the road network outside, which has grown as the demand for cars has grown. The nearby housing estates, where a large proportion of the workers live, also appear as part of the total industrial unit.

One finds very much the same at Northfield, near Birmingham, where the Austin works grew up in a similar higgledy-piggledy fashion, which is apt to baffle visitors, but appears to make sense to the people who work there. At the Ford factory at Dagenham, the situation is rather different. Here, a completely new factory was built in the 1930s, in green fields, and although there have been a number of additions and modifications since then, the site, in comparison with Cowley and Northfield, still has a planned and orderly look about it, when seen from the air. What is most remarkable about aerial photographs taken over and around the Ford plant, however, is the enormous acreage of housing estates, occupied almost entirely by Ford workers and their families. If one requires convincing visual evidence of the saying that 'Ford is Dagenham and Dagenham is Ford', photographs taken from the air supply it admirably.

Organic growth is normal in manufacturing plants, but very often the original building is completely surrounded by more recent addition and can be seen only from the air. The ideal situation, of course, would be to have a series of aerial photographs of a factory and its surroundings, taken at intervals of, say, ten years, but this is rarely achieved, even in the case of very large firms, who might be expected to do so as a matter of routine, and in practice one usually has to make do with a more haphazard range of material for study purposes.

One needs, of course, to document decline and contraction, as well as growth and expansion, and this is particularly true of the older manufacturing areas since the end of the Second World War. Two different factors have to be considered. The first is the fading away of whole industries and the second the long-overdue modernisation and replacement of plant. It is now generally admitted that by the 1950s a very high proportion of Britain's factories were obsolete and worn-out and that no amount of rehabilitation could have put the matter right. A special problem was that of the multi-storey factory, especially favoured by the textile industry. This type of factory had been constructed in the days of water- and steam-power, when the most economical method of working was to have as many working floors as possible, one above the other, in order to keep the mechanical transmission links from the water-wheel or steam-engine as short as possible. With the coming of electric motors, this was no longer necessary, and since single-storey buildings are now normal in manufacturing, it was difficult to find new owners or tenants for the old mills and many, sadly, have been pulled down, despite the great architectural merit of a number of them. With the chimneys down and the mills disappearing fast, the whole landscape of cities like Preston, Oldham and Leeds has changed, as a comparison of pre-1939 and modern aerial photographs makes very clear.

Equally far-reaching changes have taken place outside the textile areas. In the Sheffield area and in the Black Country, hundreds of acres of nineteenth-century factory buildings have been cleared away during the past thirty years and in the Potteries the disappearance of the traditional bottle-kilns over the same period has not only transformed the appearance of the district but removed a source of atmospheric pollution which made the air of the Potteries among the most smoke-laden in Britain. Much of industrial East London has gone and so, too, has a large part of Reading's manufacturing capacity, with the demolition of nearly all of Huntley & Palmer's huge biscuit-making factory, close to the centre of the town. One could continue the list for a long time.

Hand in hand with the clearance of old factory buildings has gone a widespread programme of landscape rehabilitation which has made thousands of square miles of industrial dereliction worth looking at again. Waste-tips have been levelled and covered over with soil, foul ponds have been filled in, grass sown and trees planted, so that much of the worst degradation caused by the Industrial Revolution is no longer to be seen.

One cannot say, unfortunately, that these profound changes in the appearance of Britain have been recorded as one had a right to expect. There are, of course, many before-and-after pictures, but they have been sporadic and, in many instances, accidental. Where large areas are concerned, as is usually the case, aerial photography is an essential part of the recording process, but in most instances it has not been methodically organised or commissioned by the local authorities involved. A great opportunity has been missed.

The woollen mills at Bradford-on-Avon, Wiltshire

The sixteenth century was the great age of the West of England cloth industry. During that period the clothing districts of Wiltshire, Somerset and Gloucestershire were the chief industrial concentrations in Britain. In 1565, cloth represented 78 per cent of all our exports, most of it being in the form of undyed broadcloth. The system remained virtually unchanged until the nineteenth century. The raw wool was supplied by a merchant, the clothier, to self-employed people, who spun and wove it in their homes. The cloth was then sold to the clothiers, who were responsible for fulling it and for selling it.

During the seventeenth century the West of England trade changed, and became based on the production of lighter-weight coloured broadcloths. This situation continued until the early nineteenth century, with Yorkshire taking over more and more of the production of the lower grades of cloth and the West Country concentrating on cloth of higher quality. The West of England clothiers remained reasonably prosperous, as one can see from the many fine houses they built in the main cloth-making towns, especially Painswick, Bradford-on-Avon and Trowbridge.

From *c.* 1790 onwards, the larger firms embarked on an extensive programme of mill-building and mechanisation and the domestic system of spinning and weaving died away, a process which was accompanied by a great deal of industrial unrest and emigration. At the beginning of the present century there were thirty-two cloth factories operating in Bradford-on-Avon, but all of them had closed by 1930. The industry continued a great deal longer elsewhere in the area, however, especially in Frome, where one mill was still operating in the 1960s, and in Trowbridge, where one old-established concern has managed to stay in business until the present day, mainly by concentrating on short production runs, which are of no interest to the large mills.

Photograph **26**, an exceptionally clear and useful one, shows Bradford-on-Avon as it was in 1959. Holy Trinity Church is at bottom centre, and to the left of it, across the road, is the little Saxon church of St Lawrence, with a range of weavers' cottages extending towards the right. Further along the River Avon to the left is the splendid five-storey factory, Abbey Mill, built in 1875 as a rubber mill. Its exceptionally elegant and well-proportioned chimney was an important feature of the townscape; it was foolishly truncated during the 1960s. A number of other mill-buildings can be picked out on both sides of the river, as one moves towards the top of the picture. Like practically every other building in this beautiful town, all are of stone.

The gabled riverside building just behind the rubber-mill chimney dates from 1805. It was originally a woollen mill. Beyond the bridge, there are several more mills, mostly of the late eighteenth and early nineteenth centuries.

The impressive mansion near the top centre of the picture, set within a park and a screen of trees, is The Hall, built by John Hall, a wealthy clothier,

26 Bradford-on-Avon, Wiltshire: **general view.** Cambridge University Collection, ZI 37: July 1959.

in 1616. It eventually passed into the hands of the Moulton family, who were responsible for setting up the rubber industry in Bradford-on-Avon, as a successor to the dying clothing trade. To the right of the trees, between The Hall and the river, one can see the three-storeyed Kingston Mill, with its little bell-turret. Built in 1805, it was one of the most beautiful cloth-mills in Britain and its demolition in the mid-1970s was an act of civic irresponsibility. With the disappearance of the local cloth-manufacturing industry, Kingston Mill passed into the hands of the Spencer Moulton rubber company. Later, when Spencer Moultons went out of business, all the factory buildings surrounding the chimney to the left of Kingston Mill were acquired by the Avon Rubber Company, for use by its Industrial Products Division. Avon also bought the 1875 rubber-mill, which has previously been mentioned, and have now converted it, very skilfully, into offices for the Company. The modern factory premises between Kingston

Mill and the top of the picture also belong to the Avon Rubber Company.

Photograph **27**, taken from the steep hillside on the western side of Bradford-on-Avon, has almost the effect of an aerial photograph. It shows, in the centre, Abbey Mill, and beyond it, The Hall and Kingston Mill. Given Bradford's site, this kind of photograph arouses no particular feeling of privilege, since anyone could obtain such a view merely by climbing the hillside. But a similar view of, say, Manchester or Birmingham, both built on the flat, would be exciting, because it would, to the average citizen, be abnormal.

The woollen industry was originally located along the banks of the Avon because water-power was required to drive the fulling stocks. For a short period in the late eighteenth and early nineteenth centuries, spinning and weaving machinery was also water-powered. By 1838, however, four woollen mills in Bradford-on-Avon

34

27 Bradford-on-Avon: Abbey Mill, **The Hall** and Kingston Mill. Photograph, William Morris: 1963.

were equipped with steam-engines and thereafter the main function of the Avon was as a domestic and industrial sewer, and as a source of water for washing the wool or for fulling the finished cloth. The area is very hilly, and reasonably level sites for factories were to be found only along the banks of the river. But, throughout Victorian times, the power came from coal, as the two chimneys shown in the photograph remind us.

It is interesting to observe that the seventeenth- and eighteenth-century Wiltshire clothiers built their houses close to the centre of the town where their mills were. There was no good reason why they should not do so. Before the coming of steam-power, there was no smoke, soot and dust to make life unpleasant, and to live inside a town,

especially one as agreeable as Bradford-on-Avon, enabled one to enjoy the pleasures of society more easily. A careful study of the photograph will reveal these graceful houses dotted about everywhere. During its three centuries of prosperity, Bradford-on-Avon created one of the most satisfying blends of industrial and residential buildings to be found anywhere in Britain, with everything constructed of the local stone and with no attempt either to segregate the working classes into ghettoes or to encourage the capitalists to forget the source of their income by living a long distance away from it. Bradford-on-Avon looks good partly because its industry was a clean industry and partly because everyone, of whatever social class, lived where he worked.

35

28 Trowbridge, Wiltshire: view from roof of Salter's woollen mill. Photograph, William Morris: 1963.

Trowbridge, Wiltshire: the aerial close-up

Within a thickly built-up area, a tall building can often provide many of the advantages of an aerial photograph, together with some which cannot normally be obtained from a true aerial perspective. Photograph **28** is a good case in point. It was taken in 1965, from the roof of Samuel Salter's woollen mill in Trowbridge, shown in **29**. The mill, built in 1869, was severely damaged by fire in 1931. After the fire, it was restored, with the top storey removed.

By the end of the eighteenth century, the Wiltshire handloom weavers, working in their homes, were finding it increasingly difficult to meet the competition of power-driven looms in factories. Preferring to stay independent, even with a reduced standard of living, they avoided being swept into the factory system as long as they possibly could. In Trowbridge one can see one of the methods they used to preserve their traditional way of working, large brick-built sheds put up in the back gardens of houses. In these they could accommodate two or in some instances three looms, so that the working unit was a compromise between a cottage workshop and a factory. This allowed a weaver to gain, at least for a short period, some of the advantages of concentration and size, without taking the decisive step of abandoning his independence as a master-man.

This important transitional feature of the industry can only be appreciated from above. The roof of Salter's mill provides exactly the viewing height and angle which is required.

The two splendid eighteenth-century clothiers' houses in the background are now both banks and very carefully maintained for that reason.

36

29 Trowbridge: Salter's woollen mill. Photograph, William Morris: 1963.

New Lanark, Strathclyde

New Lanark, a small village on the north-east bank of the River Clyde, a little below Corra Linn Falls, is internationally famous, because of its association with the pioneering social experiments of Robert Owen. Owen did not build New Lanark. He took it over as a going concern from David Dale, who had been in partnership with Richard Arkwright, the inventor of a cotton-spinning machine, known as the waterframe. The mills at New Lanark were built in order to exploit Arkwright's invention and it is thought that they were the first to apply water-power to spinning.

Dale built housing and had the reputation of being a model employer. He had, however, other

37

30 **New Lanark, Strathclyde.** Cambridge University Collection, BRB 10: August 1974.

business interests, and in 1799 he sold New Lanark to the New Lanark Twist Company, which had been formed to acquire the village. Owen then married Dale's daughter and went to live in New Lanark as manager. The enterprise was a commercial success under his management and he also gave much attention to improving the working conditions and education of the employees. He resigned from the position in 1828 and the property then passed through a number of hands until it came under the control of the Gourock Ropework Company, who carried out a programme of modernisation during the 1960s. These improvements, however, were confined to the mills themselves. The Company was unable to meet the cost of bringing the housing up to the standard expected today and the New Lanark Association was formed in order to raise funds for the purpose. The Association no longer functions

and the Gourock Ropework Company has severed its connection with New Lanark. The whole complex now belongs to the County Council, which is making every effort to preserve the village and to keep it alive.

The main value of **30** is that it indicates the size of the task facing any organisation which attempts to look after this huge and difficult industrial site. Traditionally, New Lanark is called a village, but, as the picture makes clear, the buildings are far from being on a village scale. The mills, on the left-hand side, are large factories and it would be difficult to use them for any other purpose, although, given their picturesque setting, it might just conceivably be possible to convert them into flats, always supposing that it were possible to find several hundred people willing to become tenants.

Whether one is thinking of the mills in the

31 New Lanark: contemporary water-colour. Photograph, James Hall (Photographers) Ltd., Greenock, B876/8.

front or the housing behind and to the right, one problem immediately presents itself – where are the residents to park their cars? New Lanark is on a wooded and steeply sloping hillside. There are no vacant spaces for more than a few cars at present and more could be provided only by felling trees and cutting into the hillside. If this were done, one would be faced with the all-too familiar situation of a new amenity destroying an old one. New Lanark was not built for a car-owning population, but it makes little sense to talk of modernising the properties unless one has a broadly based definition of 'modernisation'.

Reproduced from a contemporary water-colour, **31** shows New Lanark as it was in Owen's time. A comparison with **30** gives an idea of the changes which have taken place since. There would not have been a great deal of information which an oblique aerial photograph could have added to this, had such a possibility existed in the 1820s.

Photograph **30** reveals another equally intractable problem. Dale and Owen built multi-storey factories, because that was the most efficient way of using water-power. The water-wheels transmitted power to a system of gearing and shafting. In order to lose as little power as possible from transmission, the factory building had to be kept as compact as possible, which meant that one built upwards to the limit of the materials and structural techniques available at the time. Exactly the same considerations applied when the water-wheels were replaced by steam-engines, as happened eventually at New Lanark. The chimney and boilerhouse were demolished in the 1960s, since they were considered to conflict with the attempt to preserve the site as it was in the time of Robert Owen.

But, when the Gourock Ropework Company modernised the mills, they naturally installed electric motors to drive the machinery and removed the old belt-and-shaft driving mechanism. At that point, the design of the mills became both irrelevant and unhelpful. A multi-storey factory is more inconvenient, and more disliked by operatives, than one in which everything is on ground-floor level. This is the main reason why old textile mills all over the country have been so difficult to let or sell, and why they have been demolished in their dozens during the past thirty years, even though they were solid and well-built and in excellent structural condition. They were unwanted because they were technically outmoded.

39

32 Park Mill, Royton, Lancashire. Photair Ltd., Eccles, ref. 2330: late 1940s. Now in Cambridge University Collection.

The fact that a building is classified as being of outstanding historical and archaeological importance does nothing, alas, to alter the fact that it is obsolete. Aesthetically it may be superb, but economically it becomes more impossible with each year that passes.

A photograph of New Lanark from the air stimulates this kind of reflection and leads to the inevitable question, 'What is to happen to these beautiful buildings, of such historical importance, when no further industrial use can be found for them?' They can be preserved only if they can be used and, for this reason, they may be destined to decay and tumble into ruins, just as the civic buildings of Greece and Rome were.

One should note, by the way, the stream entering from the right and then cascading down and along the front of the mills, providing the machinery with its source of power. Factories of this size required a great deal of power, which was the reason for choosing the site in the first place.

Park Mill, Royton, Lancashire

The impossible situation in which the great nineteenth-century textile mills find themselves today is well illustrated by 32, taken at some time in the late 1940s. It shows Park Mill, Royton, in the foreground, with other Victorian cotton mills above and to the right of it. Fifty years ago there were a number of such mills in the centre of Royton, on both sides of the Rochdale Road. Only two are now functioning as textile mills. Those of the remainder which still stand are either derelict or have been adapted to other purposes. Most of the chimneys have been felled, to avoid maintenance problems.

At the time when the mills were built, they formed part of a total economic concept. The workers lived in houses close to the mill and amenities were close at hand. One can see allotments at the right centre edge of the picture and part of a park on the left edge. As a unit for living

33 British Nylon Spinners, Pontypool, Gwent. ICI Fibres archive: 1949.

and working in, Royton made sense. Cotton textiles were one of Britain's strongest industries and the owners and shareholders of factories like these could reckon to get a fair return for their investment. These handsome, solidly built factories were an expression of confidence in the industry.

During the 1950s and 1960s, the British textile industry virtually collapsed. The production of cheap fabrics, the bread and butter of the industry, shifted to countries, especially in the Far East, where labour costs were much lower than in Britain, and where the most up-to-date machinery could be installed from the beginning, in modern, single-storey buildings, which were easy to run and cheap to build and maintain. The great mills of Lancashire, six storeys and more high, like Park Mill at Royton, were unable to compete. Built for the age of steam, they were all wrong for the age of electricity. They are architecturally superb, but it is difficult to see any kind of future for them.

Only an aerial photograph can do full justice to the majestic way in which they take command of

the area and, without the chimneys, it is easy to forget why they were built so tall and so solid, able to stand up to the constant pounding and shaking of the steam-engine and of the drive-shafting which was taken to every floor and corner of the building. These factories may have shaken, but they rarely shook down. The demolition men have a great respect for them.

British Nylon Spinners, later ICI Fibres, Pontypool, Gwent

Nylon was first produced in the United States, by Du Pont, in 1937. The British manufacturing rights were bought by ICI and in 1940 British Nylon Spinners, a joint ICI–Courtauld company, was established to make nylon yarn in this country. During the war years, all manufacturing was for the Government, in temporary premises at Coventry and Stowmarket. These plants were closed in 1948 and all production was centred on British Nylon Spinners' new factory at Pontypool. This was built on the site of a large

34 ICI Fibres, Pontypool. ICI Fibres archive, A1296/68: 1968.

wartime hutted camp, which had housed people working at the nearby Royal Ordnance Factory.

The pilot plant at Pontypool was ready by the end of 1946. It was used mainly to train foremen and charge-hands until the main factory was completed. Full-scale spinning began in 1948, but demand increased so fast that between 1951 and 1953 a second factory had to be built on the site. When this, too, failed to satisfy the market, additional factories were set up at Doncaster, in 1955, and at Hucclecote, on the outskirts of Gloucester, in 1959–60.

The Company continued to prosper until the late 1960s, when it became evident that there was a serious world surplus of manufacturing capacity within the industry. One-half of what had by then become the ICI Fibres factory at Pontypool was then disposed of to other concerns.

Photographs 33 and 34 illustrate the complete Pontypool cycle. The earlier (33) was taken in 1949. The pilot plant is on the extreme right and to the left of it one can see what remained of the wartime camp. The new factory, which became operational in 1948, is on the left of the photo-graph. The tower block at the front of both the pilot plant and the 1948 building housed the equipment for drawing the continuous nylon filament, which was afterwards spun and reeled in the buildings behind.

Photograph 34, taken in 1968, shows the factory at its peak. The hutted camp has been built over and the pilot plant absorbed into a new complex of buildings. The workers were by now steadily motorising themselves and car-parks had been constructed to meet their needs.

The peak, however, was soon past. Only the 1948 section of the works is now concerned with producing nylon yarn. Everything to the right of it has been sold off and converted to other industrial uses.

Pedigree Petfoods, Melton Mowbray, Leicestershire

The market for pet foods in Britain is very large. It is estimated that about half the households in Britain own a pet of some kind and supplying

35 Pedigree Petfoods, Melton Mowbray, Leicestershire. Lithograve (Birmingham) Ltd., 1058A/2: 1958.

these pets with food has created a major industry. Britain lives increasingly on ready-prepared dishes and on snacks, which contain no waste and therefore no scraps for the dog or cat. There are many households today into which no meat bones and no fish other than fish fingers are brought. This is a post-1945 phenomenon, with great commercial possibilities, and the firm which has exploited the situation most successfully is Pedigree Petfoods.

The company has an interesting history. In 1934, an American manufacturer, Forrest E. Mars of Mars Bar fame, bought a small Manchester company, Chappel Brothers, which canned low-quality meat and sold it as dog food, under the brand name of Chappie. Mars transferred production of Chappie to the Slough Trading Estate and added a cat food, Kit-E-Kat, to the range. By the time war broke out, the business had become moderately successful.

After the War, however, a boom period began and by 1951 a move to a new site had become essential. The decision was taken to re-establish Chappie in an old sewing-thread mill at Melton Mowbray, recently vacated by Paton and Baldwin. Sales rose fast, new buildings were erected, and in 1953, in order to meet the ever-increasing demand, the factory went over to continuous shift working. In 1957 Chappie Limited became Petfood Limited and in 1974 Pedigree Petfoods. A second factory, at Peterborough, was opened in 1974. Both factories are very large, very up-to-date, and very hygienic. There would be no problem at any time in converting the Pedigree Petfoods factories to the production of foodstuffs intended for human consumption.

Melton Mowbray, a market town in the centre of a mainly agricultural district, had no previous experience of industry on this scale. One could say that it was brought sharply face to face with

43

36 **Pedigree Petfoods: a later view.** Cambridge University Collection, RC8–ER 217: August 1982. Scale 1:10,700.

the Second Industrial Revolution after missing the first. Pedigree Petfoods soon became the town's largest employer and it has continued to grow, spreading almost to the limits of the available land.

Photographs **35** and **36** illustrate the process of growth between 1958 and 1982.

In **35**, it can be seen that much development has taken place since Pedigree Petfoods arrived in Melton Mowbray in 1951. The old three-storeyed Paton and Baldwin mill is still there at bottom centre, near the railway tracks, and the factory has extended as far as the edge of the original site, the boundary being the River Wreak, which conditioned the triangular shape of the factory area. Most significant, in view of subsequent extensions, is the gasworks site on the other side of the river, where the retort house and two gasholders are still standing, the typical plant of a small-town

gasworks, surrounded by an unlovely area of dumps, stagnant water and dereliction.

Photograph **36** documents what had taken place during the succeeding twenty-four years. The Paton and Baldwin building has gone and this part of the factory has been continued to cover the whole of the site occupied in 1958 by the single-storeyed factory buildings adjoining the chimney. Even more important, however, is what the Company has achieved on the other side of the river. Everything to do with the gasworks has gone – North Sea gas had made the local production of gas obsolete and unnecessary – and a large new factory building covers practically the whole site, with a conveyor bridge linking the two sections of the factory, one on either side of the river.

As the aerial view makes evident, there is now no further room for expansion at Melton Mowbray.

44

37 Suttons Seeds at Reading, Berkshire. Archives of Suttons Seeds (now of Torquay), M.665: mid-1930s.

If the demand for pet foods continues to rise, future development will have to lie elsewhere.

The photograph also provides a clue to the considerable suspicion and hostility which Pedigree Petfoods had to face during its early days in Melton Mowbray. It can be seen that the town falls into two parts, north and south of the railway. To the north is the older district, with the shops, church, administrative offices, such industry as exists apart from Pedigree Petfoods, and estates of working-class houses. The southern section is overwhelmingly middle-class, with owner-occupied detached and semi-detached houses and substantial gardens. A high proportion of the people living here are either retired or commute to Leicester to work. Melton Mowbray has become, in fact, one of the more agreeable and fashionable dormitory areas for Leicester.

The people who bought houses south of the tracks had come to live in Melton Mowbray mainly because it was a small country town with no industry worth mentioning. If they had wanted industrial neighbours, they could have settled in Leicester and avoided the expense of commuting. The appearance of a large industrial concern on their doorstep appeared both as an intrusion and a threat, and for a long time there was a whispering campaign about the sinister activities which were

alleged to go on within the factory. Sealed boxcars of unspeakable raw materials were supposed to arrive by rail during the night and all enquiries about them were met, so it was said, with a wall of silence. The rumours were completely untrue, but it was essential for the commuters, having identified the enemy, to believe the worst about him.

To the people who lived north of the tracks, however, the arrival and growth of Pedigree Petfoods represented much-needed jobs, and for this reason they had quite a different attitude towards the firm.

Suttons of Reading, Berkshire

John Sutton established his business in Reading in 1806, dealing in corn and agricultural seeds. It prospered, and in 1858 Suttons received the Royal Warrant. The interest shown in gardening by the Victorian upper and middle class enabled Suttons to develop a profitable secondary business in flower and vegetable seeds. By the 1950s the offices, warehouses and packing buildings in the centre of Reading occupied more than 2 ha and, as real estate, the site had become extremely

45

38 **The Weetabix factory at Burton Latimer, Leicestershire.** Archive of Weetabix Ltd.: 1977.

valuable. It was, however, very congested and difficult to run. Over the years, building had been added to building and, with the steady expansion of the business, working conditions were no longer satisfactory. In 1962, therefore, the Royal Seed Establishment left its old home, having sold off the site for a very satisfactory figure and moved to new headquarters on the outskirts of the city. The old buildings were pulled down and a large part of the area which formerly belonged to Suttons is now covered by an office building put up by the Prudential Insurance Company.

It so happens that in the mid-1930s – the Company does not know the exact date – Suttons commissioned an aerial photograph of their premises. It was subsequently used for advertising purposes, with each building thoughtfully labelled. The photograph, **37**, indicates the departments into which the business was at that time organised and the size of each building gives some idea of the relative importance of the department to which it belonged.

One would have thought the fire hazard must

have been immense. The firm was evidently fully conscious of the risk and this was, indeed, one of the reasons for deciding to move elsewhere. The row of buildings in the top left-hand corner, labelled Firemen's Cottages, is significant.

The Garage might be considered rather small, even in the 1930s, for a business of this size. The Company's vans and lorries were, however, mainly employed ferrying orders to the railway station. Smaller packets and parcels were collected by the Post Office and more bulky goods, such as potatoes and farm seeds, were transported to and from Reading freight depot by the Great Western Railway, either by lorry or, more frequently, by horse-drawn waggons. Suttons did not need to have a large transport organisation of their own.

They were, incidentally, the second largest employer in Reading, the largest being Huntley and Palmer, the biscuit manufacturers. More than 500 people worked in the buildings shown in the photograph. Had there been a fire, the consequences could have been very serious.

46

39 Lec Refrigeration, Bognor Regis, West Sussex. Lec Refrigeration archives: 1946.

Weetabix at Burton Latimer, Leicestershire

Branded breakfast cereals were invented in the United States, where they underwent great commercial development during the second half of the nineteenth century. The Kellogg empire was founded in 1906 and by the end of the First World War enough British consumers had been converted to the new fashion to make production here worthwhile. Kelloggs established themselves at Trafford Park, Manchester, in the 1920s and their factory, greatly extended, is still on the same site. All the main American breakfast cereals are manufactured in Britain and some of the factories, such as that of Shredded Wheat, now Nabisco, at Welwyn Garden City, are of considerable interest to the historians of industrial architecture.

The only British-owned cereal of any consequence is Weetabix. Production began in 1932 in a disused flour mill at Burton Latimer, near Kettering. Weetabix is still made only at Burton Latimer, and since 1932 the company has obtained a 20 per cent share of the United Kingdom breakfast cereal market. A large new plant was built in 1967, but the old mill is still in use.

Photograph **38** shows the development which had taken place up to 1977. The four-storeyed mill is clearly visible in the centre of the picture, with modern silos against it on two sides. The Weetabix area occupies the bottom half of the photograph, from just behind the factory chimney to the railway line. All the buildings beyond the furthermost boundary of Weetabix are post-Second World War. Weetabix established itself in the green fields and remained in that situation, without industrial neighbours, for the first thirty years of its existence.

The nineteenth-century owners of the mill chose the site mainly because of its convenient access to the railway. Weetabix, like the adjoining factories, has no need for a rail service nowadays, so the siding to it has been closed and built over.

Lec Refrigeration, Bognor Regis, West Sussex

Lec had its beginnings in 1940, in a modest workshop at North Bersted, on the outskirts of Bognor Regis, making small parts for defence contracts. It prospered, and in 1942 it moved into

47

40 Lec Refrigeration, nearly thirty years later. Photograph, C. Howard & Son Ltd., Chichester, c75 53A: July 1975.

larger premises in Longford Road, Bognor Regis, and became registered as the Longford Engineering Company. By the end of the War, the decision had been taken to design and make refrigerators, in the belief, fully justified by events, that there was a huge pent-up demand for them. In 1946 a move was made to new buildings on the present Shripney Road site and the Longford Engineering Company became Lec. Photograph **39**, taken in 1946, shows the new building.

The Company grew fast, as an aerial photograph, **40**, taken in 1975, makes clear. The 1946 building is in the centre of the picture, south of the long white building, which is much higher than its neighbours and with cars parked in front of it. The airstrip, which was an important factor in the success of Lec, runs diagonally across the top half of the picture. Lec had a company aeroplane, with a full-time pilot, from the mid-1950s onwards. During the 1950s and 1960s, a period of intense activity by the Company, the Chairman, Managing Director and sales staff of Lec flew extensively throughout Britain and Europe, to demonstrate the firm's products and obtain orders. Without its airstrip and its aeroplane, the Company believes it would never have grown as it did.

Elstree film studios, Hertfordshire

Most of the British film studios were built between 1920 and 1935 and closed during the 1940s and 1950s. The pioneering studios were at Shepherds Bush (1914) and Lime Grove (1915). The others of note were Islington (1924); British National, at Elstree (1926); British International, also at Elstree (1927); Ealing (1930); and Denham (1934).

Elstree was built for the job, as 'the Hollywood of England'. Its predecessors had been existing buildings adapted for film-making. There were two vast, barn-like steel and asbestos structures, in which it was possible to have three productions going on at the same time. With the coming of sound films, one of these hangars was divided up with thick walls, to make three smaller sound stages. The other was left undivided, for large productions.

When the British National Company, which had built the first Elstree studios, went into liquidation, British International took over the premises and built proper sound studios. Meanwhile, Herbert Wilcox had started up his new British and Dominions Company, soon to be taken over by British International, in new buildings immediately adjoining those of British International. These studios were designed for sound from the beginning. They were unfortunately gutted by a disastrous fire in the mid-1930s, so the building one now sees there is largely a reconstruction.

Photograph **41**, taken in the autumn of 1927, shows the facilities at Elstree after the completion of British International's new studios. The British

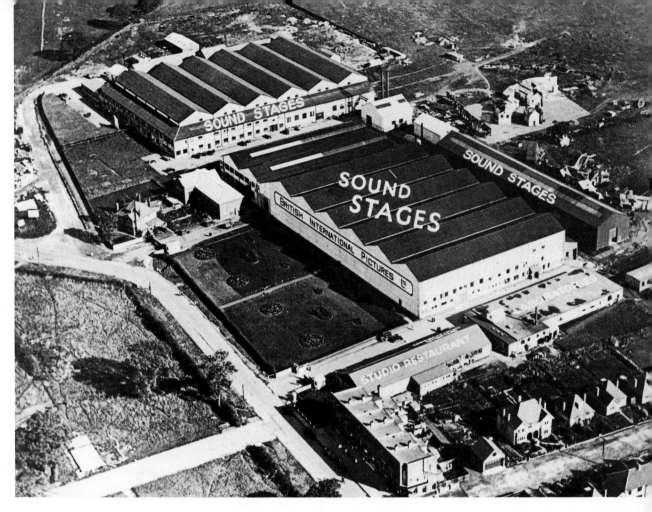

41 **Elstree film studios, Hertfordshire.** National Film Archive, 116750: 1927.

and Dominion studios are in the top left-hand corner of the picture.

The studios at Elstree, like those at Denham, were built in what was then the open country. The performers and most of the technical and administrative staff usually lived in London and travelled to and from their work by train. It was necessary to be completely self-sufficient, particularly in the provision of meals and electricity. The restaurant is marked on the photograph and the electricity was generated in the small white building with a pair of chimneys between the two sets of sound stages. Heating came from the same source. This was before the days of the National Grid and, since the electricity supplied by local companies tended to be somewhat irregular, the film companies preferred to make their own. Film processing was carried out on the premises; the building marked Laboratories shows where this was done.

The large rectangular apron of concrete to the right of the boiler house was used for outdoor sets. The one shown in position in the photograph appears to represent a street scene.

The Ford factory at Dagenham, Essex

The Ford Motor Company was set up in Trafford Park, Manchester, in 1911, to assemble parts made in the United States and in this way to supply British customers with Ford cars. Twenty years later they moved to a new factory at Dagenham. By this time the market had grown to such an extent that it was cheaper to build cars in Britain than to import them from America, especially since the British government's policy of 'imperial preference' discriminated against American imports.

Before Ford arrived in the district, Dagenham was a small Essex town. Its growth to a population of more than 50,000 is due almost entirely to Ford, which employs roughly three out of every five adult males living within 8 km of the plant.

The Ford factory at Dagenham is unique among pre-Second World War British car factories in having been planned and built as a single unit. The contrast with the British Leyland plants at Cowley and Longbridge is very striking.

49

42 The Ford factory at Dagenham, Essex. Ford Motor Company archives, 92.E. 17: 1949.

Cowley and Longbridge have grown piecemeal over a period of three-quarters of a century and now present a very heterogeneous, not to say hotchpotch appearance. Ford at Dagenham, on the other hand, still has, after fifty years, a cohesion and compactness which is markedly absent at the other two places.

Photographs **42**, taken in 1949, and **43**, taken in 1972, show what happened on the site during a period of twenty-three years of remarkable development and prosperity. There has in fact been very little change. The foundry, with its four chimneys, on the right of the picture, is much as it was, the administrative building in the centre of the river frontage is still there, and so is the curving jetty along the Thames shore. One gasholder has been demolished and two, further back on the site, have taken its place.

The principal developments appear to concern parking areas and storage buildings. In 1949 only a minority of Ford employees came to work by car, but in 1972 most of them probably did so. The large staff car park which has appeared behind the northern end of the factory buildings is interesting evidence of the motorisation of the British working class during the 1950s and 1960s.

The blast furnace, seen behind the foundry, was an unusual feature of a British motor plant. It produced pig iron for the foundry, which existed primarily in order to make cylinder blocks, which, on this site, was until recently cheaper than the normal practice of buying them from specialist suppliers. One important reason for this is that the raw materials required – iron ore, limestone and coke – could be brought directly to

43 The Ford factory, twenty-three years later. Ford Motor Company archives, 1972.1209.33: 1972.

the works by barge and coaster. In both pictures, one can see vessels being unloaded at the jetty and their cargoes taken by overhead conveyor to be tipped at the stacking yard between the factory and the blast furnace.

The old Ford works at Trafford Park, Manchester

Photograph **44** was taken in the early 1950s. It shows the former Ford plant on the far left of the group of factories. At that time, as today, the buildings were occupied by the Carborundum Company. The comparison with Ford's Dagenham plant is instructive. At Trafford Park, there was no room to expand and no opportunity to unload materials straight from coasters and barges to the blast furnaces serving the foundry that was planned.

This, as the photograph shows, is very much the old style of industrial estate. Many of the factories had their own steam-raising plant and the chimneys associated with it, and there was a network of railway tracks to provide transport facilities. At the time this photograph was taken Trafford Park, a notable pioneer in its day, had a distinctly time-worn look about it, an unmistakable image of yesterday. One can see why, in 1929, Ford felt impelled to move, although Trafford Park did not look quite like this during the time they were there.

The British Leyland works, Cowley, Oxfordshire

Herbert Austin began making motor cars at Northfield, Birmingham, in 1905. William Morris was selling his first cars in 1912. They both pros-

44 The old Ford works at Trafford Park, Manchester. Airviews Ltd., 27508: early 1950s.

pered because, unlike most of their competitors, they understood that, in order to be successful in the motor business, it was necessary to assemble components made by other manufacturers. The main skills consisted of driving as hard a bargain as possible with one's suppliers and of organising the business efficiently. It was also an advantage to have one's factory in the right place. Birmingham, Coventry and Oxford were good places to establish a car-assembly plant, because they were within easy distance of the specialist firms who supplied the components.

After some years spent developing his ideas about motor cars within the city of Oxford itself, Morris moved to Temple Cowley, a suburb of Oxford, in 1912. He first rented and then bought the buildings, which became the nucleus of a huge works. They had formerly been used as a military training college and, because they had been unoccupied for twenty-one years and were in poor condition, Morris was able to acquire them very cheaply. At the same time, he took

over the adjacent Manor House, and so was able to live close to the works during the crucial early years.

The 1914–18 War upset Morris's plans for development, but extensions to the factory began in 1919 and have continued more or less ever since. The first of the new buildings was obtained by roofing over the parade ground of the old Military College to provide a single-storey assembly area of 9,300 square metres. This building is still in use, but not for manufacturing purposes, since it is separated from the main plant by a public road.

In 1923–24 the Cowley works were producing over a quarter of the private cars made in Britain. In the following year the figure had risen to 41 per cent. Growth of this order demanded a continuous building programme and the Company bought all the adjacent land that was available. By 1939 the original 4-ha production floor area had doubled. In 1956 further planning permission was refused. The main need at that time was to

45 The British Leyland works at Cowley, Oxfordshire. Cambridge University Collection, RC8-EP 131: July 1982. Scale 1:8,000.

extend the body-building plant and the problem was solved by setting up a new plant at Swindon, instead of at Cowley.

By 1950 Morris Motors at Cowley owned 52 ha, which is about half the size of Hyde Park, and employed more than 9,000 people there. A high proportion of them lived, as their successors at British Leyland still do, on the housing estates surrounding the works.

The two overlapping photographs, **45** and **46** show almost the whole of the Cowley site. Oxford Stadium is easily recognisable in the bottom half of **45** and the railway – important up to and during the Second World War, but much less so nowadays – crosses diagonally just above the Stadium. The Oxford Eastern Bypass is the other diagonal, beginning roughly parallel with the railway and

then curving towards the centre top. The works uses practically every hectare not devoted to housing.

The disadvantages of the site are immediately obvious. The factory is awkwardly divided into four quarters by two main roads, which cross one another at the roundabout. The problem has been dealt with by means of an overhead conveyor system, which crosses two of the roads and appears in the photographs as a thick white line. The difficulties presented by Company property south of the railway are less serious, since no manufacturing is carried on here.

Had planning permission been granted, there would appear to have been only two possibilities. Either the sports ground, seen in the top right corner of both **45** and **46** would have had to be

53

46 **The British Leyland works at Cowley.** Cambridge University Collection, RC8-EP 134: July 1982. Scale 1:8,000.

surrendered and built over, or some of the agricultural land in the bottom right part of **46** would have suffered the same fate.

Nowadays, body-building is on the right-hand side of the Eastern Bypass and the remainder of the manufacturing process on the left. The principal buildings within the works are easily identified by means of the site plan (Fig. 1), but two features, not indicated on the plan, deserve special attention. One is the large proportion of the total space which has to be given up to parking cars, either those belonging to employees or those just manufactured and waiting for shipment. If some other means could be found of dealing with this, by either multi-storey or underground parking, the problem of finding additional factory areas would seem to be on the way to being solved. The second point of particular interest is the location

of the original 1912 factory. It can be seen at the top left of **45** at the corner of the building marked Tuning on the plan. Hollow Way meets Garsington Road at this point. The Military College was on Garsington Road and the dark-coloured building behind it, Tuning, is the roofed-over parade ground. All the rest of the works, the Morris empire, grew from this point.

Tyre manufacturing at Fort Dunlop, Birmingham, West Midlands

The Dunlop Rubber Company was set up in 1901, mainly in order to make bicycle tyres. The 1914–18 War necessitated a great increase in the production of solid tyres for lorries, and manufacturers were forced to operate on an altogether

54

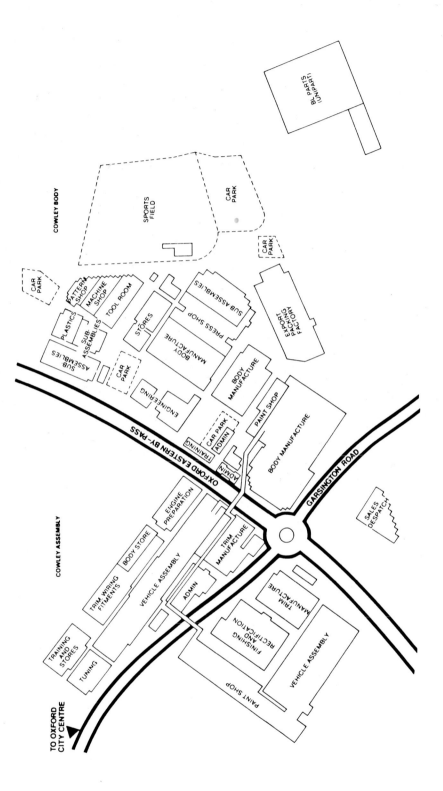

Fig. 1 Site plan of the British Leyland works at Cowley. British Leyland, neg. no. 312849.

47 **Tyre works at Fort Dunlop, Birmingham, West Midlands.** Fort Dunlop Central Photographic Unit, 27530B: 1975.

different scale and to make heavy capital investment. The most notable symbol of this was Fort Dunlop, built by the Dunlop Company in 1916 on a 120-ha site to the east of Birmingham.

Fort Dunlop was evidence that the manufacture of motor-vehicle tyres had become an important industry in its own right. The Company grew as the motor industry grew and Fort Dunlop remained an apparently unshakeable British institution until the early 1970s. From then on, the number of foreign cars imported into Britain began to increase rapidly, and very few of these cars were fitted with British tyres. The period since 1975 has been one of steady decline for Dunlop and in 1983 the Company sold out to the Japanese, who almost immediately announced their intention of closing Fort Dunlop. By 1985 tyre production may well have come to an end at Fort Dunlop.

Photograph **47** shows the works as it was in 1975, with the M6 motorway under construction just to the south of it. Fort Dunlop stretches right across the picture, the largest tyre factory outside the United States. If the British motor industry had been able to meet the challenge of foreign imports, if eighty per cent of the vehicles travelling along the M6 were British, Fort Dunlop would in all probability still be thriving.

Oil refining at Fawley, Hampshire

In 1921 the Atlantic, Gulf and West Indies Oil Company bought 270 ha of land at Fawley, on Southampton Water, and started to build a small refinery. Two years later, British–Mexican Petroleum bought out Atlantic, Gulf and West Indies, and in 1926 they in turn were taken over by the Anglo-American Oil Company, now Esso.

Fawley was originally planned to provide ship-bunkering facilities and to manufacture bitumen for road surfaces. Despite extensions, the capacity had only reached 600,000 tonnes of crude oil by 1939, when the United Kingdom's annual demand

56

48 Oil refinery at Fawley, Hampshire. An Esso photograph, Esso Petroleum Company, CAG 354: 1935.

had reached nine million tonnes. During the Second World War, refining ceased at Fawley, although it continued as a storage depot and served as an important link in the PLUTO (Pipeline Under the Ocean) network, which took fuel across the Channel to the allied forces in Europe after D-Day. The refined oil for British wartime needs continued to be imported, as it had been in peacetime, mainly from the United States, and it was paid for in dollars.

The War, and Britain's consequent shortage of dollars, changed the pattern of the oil industry. From now on, there were strong economic reasons why refining should be carried out here and not abroad. Fawley, Britain's first major oil refinery, was developed for this reason. The site was ideal, since Southampton Water provided a deep and sheltered anchorage for large ocean-going tankers, and it was a simple matter for coastal tankers to carry the refinery's products to storage depots around the coast of Britain. A further 1,200 ha of land were acquired and construction of the new refinery began in 1949.

Since the 1950s, oil has provided the basic

ingredients for a wide range of manufactured products, such as synthetic rubbers, detergents, paints and fertilisers. In 1958 the first chemical plant was built at Fawley, owned and operated by the Esso Petroleum Company. In 1966, a new associate company, the Esso Chemical Company, was formed to handle this side of the business.

Since 1973, with greatly increased prices and resulting economies in the use of oil, the demand for oil in the United Kingdom has decreased. It is now, in 1983, only 60 per cent of the 1973 total. This has necessarily changed the pattern of operations at Fawley. Some of the least economic units have been closed and others modified to allow for more efficient working, although Fawley is still the largest refinery in Britain.

Photograph **48** shows the refinery as it was in 1935, while **49** gives an impression of the same part of the site forty years later. This part of the plant is concerned wholly with storage and refining. The chemical side of the business is concentrated in an area off the left-hand side of the photograph, towards Southampton. Very little of the pre-1939 installations now remains.

49 Oil refinery at Fawley, forty years later. An Esso photograph, Esso Petroleum Company, CAG 788: 1975.

Lubricating oil at Shell Haven, Essex

Before the First World War the London and Thames Oil Company established importing, storage and refining facilities at a Thames-side site which became known as the London and Thames Haven Oil Wharves. In the early 1920s the Shell Oil Company constructed a separate refinery close to the one which was operated by London and Thames. Their installations were called Shell Haven. Towards the end of the Second World War, Shell built a specialised plant at Shell Haven for the production of lubricating oil – 'luboil' in the oil business. This plant was shut down in 1969 after twenty-five years of operation, but it was preserved intact and re-opened in the following year, to meet a shortage of lubricating oil for motor vehicles and industry. It finally closed five years later and the site was cleared. Meanwhile, in 1969, Shell had bought the London and Thames business, and the whole area is now referred to as Shell Haven, a source of some confusion for the industrial historian.

Photograph 50, taken in 1958, clarifies the situation. The Shell refinery and luboil plant, together forming Shell Haven, occupy the top left area, beyond the winding stream and open

fields. Everything on this side of them belonged to the London and Thames Haven. Subsequently, in 1978, a new luboil blending plant was built on the open ground between the two refineries.

It is very difficult to obtain any clear overall impression of an oil refinery, except from the air, since even in the case of a plant of modest size, the area covered is large and the relation between different parts of the enterprise makes little sense to an observer on the ground. The complexity of this type of manufacturing unit is illustrated by 51, taken in 1970 from the top of one of the taller pieces of equipment at Shell's luboil plant. It provides what might perhaps be described as a semi-aerial view. To the uninitiated, the site appears to be a mere jumble of pipes and tanks, but Shell's archives reveal that in the foreground of the picture one is looking at the paraffin wax plant, in the centre at the extraction unit for lubricating oil and the rewaxing unit, and in the background at the section where lubricating oils were subjected to what is technically known as the clay contacting process.

No equipment in the oil industry has a long life, partly because technological change makes much of it rapidly obsolete and partly because of the gradual corrosion which affects everything in

50 Shell refinery and luboil plant, Shell Haven, Essex. Shell photograph, HIS 108 (Historical): 1958.

51 General view of luboil plant, Shell Haven. Shell photograph, E164-377 caf.: 1970.

contact with oil and oil products. For these two reasons, the preservation of old oil refineries as technical monuments is rarely practicable. The archaeology of the oil industry is short-lived and the photographic record is consequently of great importance.

Industrial estates

Nineteenth-century factories were built more or less where it suited their owners to have them. Urban planning did not extend beyond city centres and the better-class residential areas, and industrial development was carried out in a very individualistic manner. The transport of raw materials, coal and finished or part-finished goods made easy access to canals, rivers and railways important, so there tended to be a considerable concentration of factories in those parts of a city where these services were closest at hand, which usually happened to be low-lying areas. Since each factory had its chimney, the factory districts were, in the days of steam-power, inevitably dirty, smoky and, from a residential point of view, unpleasant. The further one could live away from the factories, the better; and the more money one had, the easier it was to achieve this.

So long as factories, steam-engines, railways and dirt were inseparable, the hands of the planners were tied. In our own century, however, a completely new concept became possible. It by no means ignored railways but it was based on the availability of electric power and motor transport, which meant that one had much greater freedom in the location of industry. Given this freedom, it was possible to take a completely new site, to lay out roads and install water, gas, sewerage and electricity, and then persuade manufacturing concerns to establish themselves there. Such areas became known as industrial estates and, although they did not really become popular until after the Second World War, few towns in Britain are now without something of the kind.

Ironically, the pioneering industrial estate, at Trafford Park, on the outskirts of Manchester, was begun in 1896, when industry still depended on railways and steam-engines. There were 485 ha available, with the Manchester Ship Canal running along one side and the river along the other. The estate authorities laid out a network of service roads and railway sidings and a few years later, in 1902, a power station was built and a tramway system installed to take workers to and from Manchester. Many well-known firms, including Metropolitan Vickers, the Ford Motor Company, Kelloggs and Thomas Hedley, the soap manufacturer, have been associated with Trafford Park. They leased their sites from the estate and built the kind of premises they required.

Slough followed a different pattern. It was set up by the Government in 1929, to help to create local employment during the early years of the Depression. It had originally been a depot for the disposal of surplus First World War stores and equipment. Prospective tenants were offered roads and other services and factories of a standard size and extremely utilitarian design. Since 1945, many of the original factories have either been rebuilt or given a welcome face-life.

The Treforest and Team Valley Estates, both opened in 1936, were somewhat improved versions of the Slough model, but the Gloucester Trading Estate, created in 1964, had a different policy. It took over a 170-ha site belonging to the Hawker Siddeley Group. The Gloucester Estate is an entirely private venture and provides factory and warehouse accommodation for more than forty companies. It differs from previous industrial estates in having a comprehensive system of central services, which are offered to tenants more cheaply than if they were organised individually. These include heating, compressed air, security, canteen facilities, maintenance and medical attention for employees.

Industrial estates are difficult to comprehend from the ground. One can see the separate parts, but not the whole. With the help of aerial photographs, not only does the overall extent of the estate become apparent, but so also do the size and density of its buildings and its relationship to the local transport system and to the town itself. One can also notice the difficulties which the older estates have had in providing parking spaces for the people who now work there. The pre-1939 estates were planned on the assumption that employees would travel to work by public transport, by bicycle or on foot. Car-parking space was not included in the original layout, and as one can see from above, it has been far from easy to provide it since.

52 The Slough Trading Estate, Berkshire. Aerofilms Ltd., 15084: 1948.

Slough Trading Estate, Berkshire

Slough provides a good example of the twentieth-century pattern of industrial development. It was an estate without railway sidings and without factory chimneys, established by the Government in 1929 in an attempt to create local employment. It had been constructed immediately after the First World War for the disposal of surplus military stores. There were roads, water, sewers and electricity, and single-storey buildings of standard size and construction available to tenants whose business was considered suited to the kind of accommodation offered, that is, to light industry. The result was fairly efficient, but the general appearance of the estate could hardly be described as exciting.

Since 1945, many of the original buildings have been given a face-lift or pulled down and rebuilt. Many of the units are now much larger and the estate has largely lost the uniformity which characterised it for the first twenty years of its existence.

Photographs **52** and **53** were taken from a similar direction, **52** in 1948 and **53** in 1960 (almost certainly from a helicopter). In both pictures, the only factory chimneys to be seen are the two belonging to the power station. Another feature to strike the eye immediately is the very small amount of car-parking available at both dates. The workers of 1929 did not have cars and the only way in which this facility could be provided for the workers of today would be to demolish some of the factories and not replace them. This, however, would mean a loss of income for the estate, and since this could not be contemplated, the situation remains unchanged.

When one studies **52** it is evident that a high proportion of the original factories have already been replaced. There is a row of them along the railway, the Western Region main line from London to Swindon, and another group near the

61

53 The Slough Trading Estate. *Windsor, Slough and Eton Express*, 2812/P/D: 1960.

centre of the picture. Nearly all the others have gone, their place being taken by much larger buildings. What was envisaged in the 1920s as an estate to meet the needs of fairly small businesses has now become over the years the home of considerably larger concerns.

One could certainly say that Slough Trading Estate is using its area more economically and more profitably now. As the photograph shows, the old pattern of small individual factories involved leaving a good deal of space around and between the buildings. With the new generation of factories, these subsidiary roadways and pathways have been built over and put to profitable use.

Photograph **53** shows that the estate has expanded since **52** was taken. Many new buildings have gone up along the bottom of the picture, and there has also been development to the left of the power station. Since 1960, the process of modernisation has continued steadily. All the old buildings, except those immediately adjoining the railway, have now disappeared and the great

majority of the factories are now post-1945. For all its reputation for dreariness and monotony, Slough is situated conveniently close to London and to the motorway. Industrialists like it, even if Sir John Betjeman did not.

One can see from **52** that Slough Trading Estate has a great many houses close to it and this is indeed one of the great virtues of a modern industrial estate – it does not make a nuisance of itself. Its industries are of a kind which do not pollute the atmosphere and deposit soot along clotheslines. Industrial estates can be translated 'light industrial estates'. Slough may offend one's vision, but it causes no harm to the other four senses.

Gloucester Trading Estate

The Gloucester Trading Estate was established in 1964 to take over the complex of aircraft hangars and manufacturing facilities, some dating back to the 1914–18 War, which belonged to the Hawker

54 The Hawker Siddeley aircraft factory, Hucclecote, Gloucester. Photograph by Russell Adams, FRCPS, Gloucester, P.283/52: 1952.

Siddeley Group. The estate is a private venture and provides factories and warehouses for more than forty companies. It differs from most other industrial estates in its system of central services – heating, compressed air, security, canteens, maintenance and medical attention – which are offered to the tenants more cheaply than they could obtain or organise them individually.

Photograph **54** shows the aircraft factory as it was in 1952, before conversion to the Trading Estate began. The factories still have their wartime camouflage on them. Photograph **55** was taken at some time in 1971, **56** in 1976, and **57** in 1982. Photograph **57** gives an excellent view of the Trading Estate and of the area within which it is situated. The place is Hucclecote, once a small village and now a suburb of Gloucester. The M 5 motorway runs along the left-hand edge of the picture and the Trading Estate lies to the right of it. The former Hawker Siddeley factory occupied nearly all the buildings shown in the picture, but those used by the central services – the restaurant, medical centre and so on – on the right of the factories have been added by the Estate Company.

The large factory on the right of the Trading

Estate in **56** is that of ICI Fibres. It produces nylon yarn and was converted from a wartime aero-engine factory run by Bristol Siddeley. During the Second World War this factory and the one which became the nucleus of the Gloucester Trading Estate shared the same runway. The short taxiing runway leading off to what is now ICI Fibres is clearly visible. The Bristol Siddeley factory was built in 1939 on a golf course. After the war, it was used to build prefabricated houses. Two of these were erected by the side of the former clubhouse of the golf course and are still standing and occupied. They can just be distinguished by the side of the lane running alongside ICI Fibres, surrounded by trees. Photograph **58**, taken in 1939, shows the future ICI Fibres factory as it was in its wartime days as an aero-engine factory. No aerial photograph could have done justice to its utilitarian squalor. Photograph **59** gives an impression of how the converted and refronted factory looked in the winter of 1975.

Photograph **56**, taken obliquely, adds further details. The central boiler house, with its four chimneys, is in the centre of the complex. To the right, with curved roofs, are five aircraft hangars

63

55 The Gloucester Trading Estate, Hucclecote, Gloucester. Photograph by Russell Adams, FRCPS, Gloucester, 157/71/B: 1971.

surviving from the First World War. They have elaborate wooden roof trusses and merit preservation as technical monuments. Nowadays they are used as warehouses. New warehouses have been built between them and the airstrip. The administration block is the large E-shaped building between the boiler house and the trees.

One understands very well from this photograph why trading estates are called trading estates. It is because they contain both factories and warehouses, and a single word is required to cover both. This particular estate is exceptionally intelligently laid out. It works well because it is compact and not too big. The central services

function and are popular because they are only a short walking distance from any work-point. The centralised heating system is efficient, because the pipe-runs are not too long. Cars can be kept outside the estate, where they would be a nuisance, and left in the car park on the perimeter, because in two to three minutes on foot one is at any point on the estate.

And, always a strong selling-point, the motorway is only a stone's throw away. The aerial photograph has become an advertising weapon and many firms do indeed make use of it for precisely this purpose.

56 The Gloucester Trading Estate. Photograph by Russell Adams, FRCPS, 222/76/2-1: 1976.

57 The Gloucester Trading Estate. Cambridge University Collection, RC8–ER 124: July 1982. Scale 1:13,400.

58 The former Bristol Siddeley aero-engine factory before conversion to a nylon-spinning plant. ICI Fibres Ltd.: October 1939.

59 The converted and refronted factory of 58 as it appeared in the winter of 1975. ICI Fibres archive: 1975.

Inland waterways

Without rivers, the Industrial Revolution would have been much delayed, because the early manufacturing places – factories is too precise and modern a term – would have had no power to drive their machinery. To see the sites and the surviving buildings of these mills and workshops by the side of their source of power is consequently to see them given meaning, to make sense of their location. With the isolated large mill, at Cromford, in Derbyshire, for instance, to look at the site on ground level is to understand it without too much difficulty – a big, fast-flowing river provided adequate power to drive several water-wheels – but where a number of mills were situated at intervals of 400 m or less along a stretch of river, as in the Stroud Valley in Gloucestershire, or on the Frome in Somerset, one needs to be able to look down on a kilometre or so of the river, with the mills spaced out along it, to appreciate how wonderfully ingenious our ancestors were in taking full advantage of what seems today to be a very restricted water supply.

It is useful, too, when surveying a district by means of aerial photographs, to try to imagine how heavy materials, especially stone, were brought considerable distances in flat-bottomed boats or on rafts along a network of what are no more than streams. To read, for instance, about stone, being brought for the construction of Ely Cathedral 'by water' may suggest a sizeable river, but when one is able to see the actual watercourses which must have done the job, one is in a better position to understand how patient, adaptable and expert people in the Middle Ages were.

A phrase such as 'canalisation' is clear enough – an awkward length of river was bypassed by means of a canal, so that rapids or sharp bends or the worst effects of a tidal river could be avoided – but an aerial photograph allows one to see what was actually involved and how sensible a solution the piece of canal was. But canals do not dig themselves and, whether the artificial channel is only a hundred metres long or several kilometres, as at Exeter, it was dug out by pick-and-shovel labour, an achievement which somehow seems more impressive when one is looking at it from above, with what men did remarkably quickly running

more or less alongside what Nature had done a great deal more slowly.

Few of Britain's canals were ever a commercial success even before the railways arrived to take over their trade and, from the air, one sees both the impossibility of the competition and the tragedy of such prodigious efforts and such optimistic investment leading to such pitiful results. Both the canals and the railways naturally chose the most level ground they could find, which in many cases meant following the river valleys. Sometimes, as along much of the Kennet and Avon Canal, the railway and the canal run parallel for miles, but often they are some distance apart and it is only from the air that one can bring them into the same focus. In many cases, as with the Taunton and Exeter and the Chard canals, the canal has been completely abandoned for many years, and, with no towpath to walk along and with no road running nearby, it is now almost impossible, except from the air, to see what the route was.

Some of the greatest achievements of the canal engineers can now only be appreciated from the air. The remarkable staircase of locks which takes the Kennet and Avon up to Devizes, for example, is so long that, standing by the side of them, one can keep only two or three of them in vision at a time. An aerial photograph, however, can show the whole grand sweep of them, from bottom to top, vastly impressive, even in their present ruinous condition. It can also indicate the route of a tunnel which a boat can no longer pass through, usually because of fallen masonry. Canal tunnels, unlike railway tunnels, rarely ran very far below the surface and, where the use was unavoidable, they were nearly always excavated by means of what might be termed holes in the roof. The excavated material was dumped round the top of the shaft and, after the job had been completed, the hole was sealed with masonry and the heap covered over with soil. Sometimes the landowner would insist, as a condition of allowing the canal to cross his property, that the line of hillocks above the tunnel should be planted out with trees, which makes the task of following the tunnel from the air even easier than usual.

69

60 The river system in central Bristol. Cambridge University Collection, RC8–EO 226: July 1982. Scale 1:12,000.

But it is perhaps in built-up areas that one is most grateful for aerial photographs of the canal system, partly because in such places the route of the canal can be extremely difficult, and in some places impossible, to follow on foot, and partly because, where the towpath does exist, it often takes one through extremely insalubrious areas, where one would certainly not go for pleasure. The canals running through Birmingham fulfil all these conditions, and there are some nasty stretches in Manchester and Leeds, too.

With canals, as with railways, aerial photographs can be of great value in showing not only what, but why. To see a canal, even if now abandoned, close to old coal-tips is to remind oneself that its original purpose was to provide a cheap way of getting the coal from the pits to the manufacturing towns which were anxious to buy it; and to notice,

in Staffordshire, how the canal banks are lined with pottery works, now mostly disused, is to understand the point of the canal in the first place, to bring coal and raw materials in and to take finished products out. One can, of course, get the point from the ground, but what the aerial photograph adds is the dimension of quantity – the canal served not one pottery, but dozens.

Canal-building on a serious scale dates in Britain from the 1750s. Before that date, rivers had been much used for transport and on some of them artificial cuts had been made to shorten journeys and locks built to make them more easily navigable. Between 1755 and 1805, about 5,000 km of canals were added to the existing 1,600 km of navigable rivers. After 1850, very little was done to extend or improve the system, although Britain's largest canal, the Manchester Ship

70

Canal, was opened as late as 1894. It was the first and the only canal in the country to have been constructed by mechanical excavators, instead of men with spades and wheelbarrows.

The river system in central Bristol, Avon

It is very difficult to understand Bristol's rivers except from the air. Photograph 60 is a helpful reference document (north is at the top).

Until the mid-thirteenth century, Bristol was served by two rivers. The Avon ran into the city from the Bath direction and the Frome, a much lesser waterway, from Gloucestershire. The two met just below Bristol Bridge, in the top right-hand corner of the photograph. The Avon, which is conveniently dark in the photograph, runs under Bristol Bridge and off the photograph to the left, to Avonmouth and the sea.

The original Port of Bristol was to the east of Bristol Bridge, on the northern side of the river, just below the castle walls. But, by the thirteenth century, Bristol Bridge had become a serious obstacle to all but very small ships, and during that century new quays were constructed along Welsh Back and Redcliffe Back, the two sides of the straight stretch of river which runs parallel to the right-hand edge of the photograph between Bristol Bridge and Redcliffe Bridge to the south.

By the time that had been done, however, progress had overtaken the planners. Bristol's sea-going trade, especially with France and Ireland, had grown so much that a new port had become essential. What was decided was to turn the course of the Frome, so that, instead of joining up with the Avon near Bristol Bridge, it did so considerably further west. This gave a straight length of river, parallel to Welsh Back, and the half-mile of man-made waterway provided in this way became the new Port of Bristol. It was completed in 1248 and the old channel of the Frome was then filled in and built over. The northern end of the new cut, however, can no longer be seen. It was covered over in two stages, 1892–3 and 1938–9, to form what is now known as The Centre. North of this, the Frome runs through a culvert, not emerging to view again until just before Eastville.

During the following centuries the great growth in Bristol's trade once more produced intolerable congestion in the Port, and, as ships became steadily bigger, it became more and more difficult to sail them up and down the winding river between Bristol and the sea. Various palliatives were attempted, but with little success, and in 1802 the City agreed to William Jessop's radical solution to the problem.

Jessop's plan was to dam the Avon about 1.5 km due east of Redcliffe Bridge, on the Bath side of where Temple Meads railway station is now, and to dig a canal to bring the Avon back into its main course at Hotwells, about 3 km further on towards the sea. By constructing locks across the Avon at this point, a floating harbour was made available and ships entering it no longer found themselves stranded on the mud at low tide. Fresh water entered the Floating Harbour from the Frome and from a new Avon bypass, the 1.5-km Feeder Canal, which cut across a bend of the Avon to the east of Rownham (see Fig. 2). The New Cut appears grey on the photograph, running south of the Floating Harbour and approximately parallel to it.

Jessop's scheme was completed in 1809 and for the next seventy years, until Avonmouth began to enter the situation, the Floating Harbour was almost the entire Port of Bristol (see Fig. 3).

It should perhaps be mentioned that all the works described above were carried out by hand labour. The New Cut was especially difficult, since it had to be excavated through hard sandstone.

The Caledonian Canal at Fort Augustus, Highland

The Highlands of Scotland are cut across by a great natural cleft, which runs from sea to sea and passes through Inverness, Fort Augustus and Fort William in almost a straight line. Of the total distance of 180 km, 145 consist of sea and freshwater lochs, so that, in order to provide a through route for ships, only 35 km of canal had to be constructed. With such a canal available, shipping could avoid the difficult and often dangerous passage around the north of Scotland through the Pentland Firth. Thomas Telford was given the contract to build it and the canal was finally opened to traffic in 1847.

The construction of the locks at Fort Augustus was particularly difficult. The bottom lock had to be sunk well below the level of Loch Ness, and constant pumping was needed during the building work. Even after it was finished there was trouble. The entire side wall of this lock caved in and had to be rebuilt.

The photograph, 61, shows the canal and the town as they looked in 1958. The locks and the towpath have been well maintained and are in good condition. The pairs of circles by the side of each lock-gate are the tracks of the feet of people operating the mechanism to open and shut the gates.

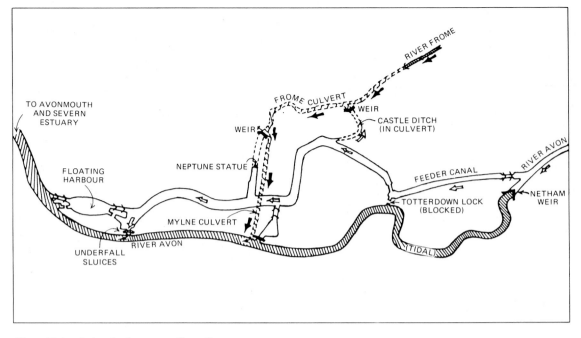

Fig. 2 Bristol city docks: water-flow diagram.

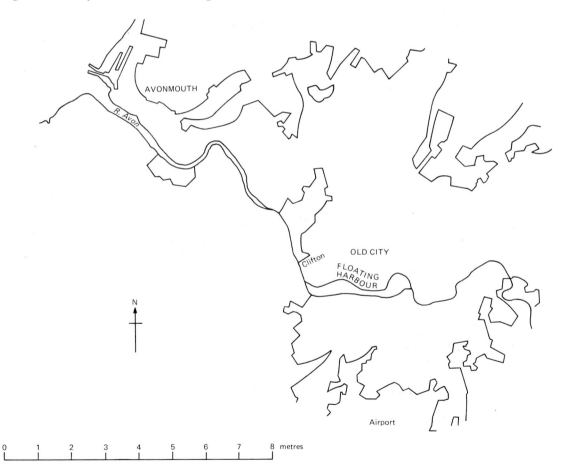

Fig. 3 Bristol: sketch showing position of city docks, Avonmouth and airport.

61 The Caledonian Canal at Fort Augustus, Highland. Cambridge University Collection, XE 45: July 1958.

The Kennet and Avon locks at Devizes, Wiltshire

The Kennet and Avon canal was opened to traffic in 1810, as a means of providing inland water transport between Bristol and London. It is 40 feet wide and in its total length of 57 miles it has 79 locks. These include the remarkable chain of 29 through Devizes, the second longest flight in Britain. Each lock is 74 feet long. The locks are built along a stretch of 2½ miles of the canal, 17 of them being in a direct line, 75 feet apart and each with a rise of 8 feet. The locks had to be supplemented with individual ponds in order to provide sufficient reserves of water when the traffic was heavy. The whole flight of locks lifts the canal 239 feet and, under normal conditions, the passage could be accomplished in three hours.

73

62 **Locks on the Kennet and Avon canal at Devizes, Wiltshire.** Cambridge University Collection, UO 18: April 1957.

The Kennet and Avon is being rehabilitated but, after so many years of neglect, the task is inevitably expensive and it may well be that the Devizes locks will be the last section to be completed. Much restoration work on the canal has been carried out since 1976 as part of the Government's Job Creation programme. In 1978 £132,000 was allocated to restore the lock chambers of the Devizes flight, but this work has not yet been carried out.

The aerial photograph, **62**, shows very clearly what a remarkable engineering project the locks were and how great the task of restoring them will be, even with the help of modern machinery. The supply ponds have become filled in and would need to be re-excavated before the locks could be guaranteed to function at all times, and the replacement of so many lock gates is a daunting task, without considering what it would cost to put the masonry of the lock chambers to rights.

The photograph provides, as a bonus, an

excellent opportunity to compare three different methods of transport, all serving the same community. The canal appears to be the most complicated, a major feat of planning as well as of engineering. Between each of the six locks at the Devizes end of the chain there is a large basin, with another linking the lock near the bottom edge of the picture with the first lock on the ladder. These basins were a very prudent provision, and necessary as a means of evening out the flow of traffic at times when the canal was under pressure. They could be termed canal sidings, parking places for boats.

To the right of the canal is the main Melksham–Devizes road and to the right again the track of the Trowbridge–Devizes railway, which branched off at Holt Junction, south of Melksham. Opened in 1857, the line was closed little more than a hundred years later. When the photograph was taken, the railway did not have long to live. The length of it which is shown here illustrates the ingenious

63 Crick tunnel, Northamptonshire. Cambridge University Collection, AZU 13: October 1969.

methods of the Victorian railway builders. What was removed from the cutting was used as part of the material employed to construct the embankment.

Crick tunnel, Northamptonshire

Crick tunnel, in Northamptonshire, forms part of the route of the Grand Union Canal. The construction of the Grand Union was authorised in 1810, to provide a link with the Leicester Union and the Grand Junction. The canal had had a chequered history. The Union Canal Bill had passed through Parliament in 1793 and work had begun from the Leicester end in the following year. There were difficulties caused by local opposition to the proposal to take the canal through Foxton and extra expense, which had not been anticipated, in driving an 800-metre tunnel to the south-west of Kitworth. The company ran out of funds and the work was stopped at Debdale. A new company, the Grand Union, took over in 1810 and completed the job.

The remaining stretch involved the construction of two substantial tunnels, at Bosworth and Crick, respectively 800 m and 1,200 m long. The contracts were given to Pritchard and Hoof of Kings Norton, who carried out much similar work elsewhere. The correspondence concerning one of these contracts, says L.T.C. Rolt, 'dispels the notion that large-scale civil engineering contracting was a product of the railway building age'.[1] Such a contract involved 'excavating the ground for the Tunnel, putting in necessary timbers, winding the spoil to the surface, loading into ships and lowering the bricks, mortar and other materials, bricking the tunnel with such strength of work as the Resident Engineer may think proper, setting and taking down the centres, drawing the timbers and pumping the water'.[2]

The tunnel at Crick was completed in 1814. Its route is indicated by the line of spoil-heaps shown on **63**. The heaps cross the picture diagonally from left centre in the direction of the top right-hand corner. The canal emerges from the tunnel in the middle of a belt of trees to the right of Crick village.

It will be noticed that the heaps of earth are very close together. This is an indication that the tunnel does not run far below the surface. If the material that was removed had not been so soft, a cutting might just have been possible. As it was, the sides of anything other than a shallow cutting would either have fallen in and been constantly troublesome, or would have had to be graded to such a slight angle that an unreasonable width of ground would have been required. Had the tunnel been deeper or if the rock had been hard, the shafts through which the excavated material was drawn to the surface would, for economic reasons, have been spaced considerably further apart.

Within a very few years, the techniques which had been learnt in building the second, nineteenth-century, wave of canal tunnels were transferred to the construction of railway tunnels. In some cases, the same experienced men were available to carry out the work.

In this same picture, one is able to observe the care which the canal surveyors took to follow the contours of the land, in order to keep construction costs to a minimum. After leaving the tunnel, the canal continues in a straight line for about 800 m, and then takes a right-angled turn to the left, so avoiding the expense of a cutting or locks.

It is curious, incidentally, that in the more than a century and a half since the spoil-heaps appeared in their fields, farmers appear to have made no attempt to remove these not inconsiderable obstacles to cultivation. At one time, the task would have demanded much time and energy but, with modern earth-moving plant, it could be accomplished very quickly and cheaply. One suspects, for this reason, that these particular items of canal archaeology may not be in existence for a great deal longer.

References

1. *Thomas Telford*, 1958, p. 164.
2. *Ibid.*

Ports and docks

For very good reasons, members of the general public are usually not allowed to wander about port areas. Ports are dangerous places for the inexperienced, with a great deal of movement taking place, and they are also excellent hunting-grounds for thieves. So security tends to be strict, unaccompanied visitors are discouraged and, apart from the men who work in the docks, very few people have any real idea of the extent and layout of the area which lies the other side of the wall. Consequently, an aerial photograph of the docks at, say, Southampton or Liverpool, is likely to reveal many surprises, even to those who have visited these places or possibly sailed from them.

Comparative photographs are essential, if one is to understand what has happened to a port over several decades. In some instances, of which the Port of London is the most notable example, one will be documenting the story of decline and abandonment. Even twenty years ago, when one took the boat down the Thames from Westminster or Tower Pier to Greenwich, there were plenty of ships moored down both sides of the river and the guide was kept busy telling passengers where each vessel came from and what kind of cargo it was unloading. Now the once thriving Port of London is dead. Its docks are in the process of being filled in or converted into floating museums or what the estate agents call 'amenity lakes', and its warehouses demolished or converted into expensive flats.

It is fashionable to blame the trade unions for what has happened, but aerial photographs quite literally put the situation into perspective. In London, Bristol, Falmouth, and many other places one can see from the air what the root cause of the trouble was. The docks were conceived and built at a time when the average merchant ship was much smaller than it is today and when all ships were unloaded either by crane or by men carrying loads on their backs or, if grain was involved, by suction pumps. The goods went from the ship into waiting railway trucks or into warehouses and cold stores, and the docks had been planned on this assumption.

As soon as containers came into the picture, many of the old-established ports were doomed. They did not have the space to store the containers after they were unloaded or waiting for shipment. Unless it is handling bulk cargoes, like ore or oil, where specialised facilities are involved, a modern port requires a very large acreage for stacking and manoeuvring containers and for parking motor vehicles which have been imported or which are destined for export. If a port was unable to provide this reasonably close to where the ships berthed, its prosperity was at an end. The congestion of buildings and traffic at the old type of port leaps to the eye from an aerial photograph.

So, too, does the actual amount of shipping in the port, and its character. The changes in both these respects have been enormous, but they are not always quite what they seem. There may, at any one time, be fewer ships in the Port of Liverpool or Southampton today than there were half a century ago, but they are bigger ships and, since wages are much higher and the investment much greater than it used to be, there is every incentive to get a vessel loaded or unloaded and turned round as quickly as possible. A ship moored at her berth is earning no money and, since modern equipment allows cargoes to be transferred from ship to shore and from shore to ship much more quickly nowadays, a well-managed ship spends a much greater proportion of the 365 days in the year at sea and far fewer days in port. But, conversely, assembling cargoes for shipment and moving them away after they have arrived occupies more of a port's time than it used to. One could express this change as an Irishism, by saying that a great deal more shipping takes place on shore today than during the 1940s and 1950s.

Another major change, very clearly shown on aerial photographs, is the virtual disappearance of the passenger liner. One has to read this from the picture in conjunction with the port buildings which existed to serve the travelling public – the rather grand terminal which served as a reception centre for passengers and their baggage and for immigration and Customs formalities, the large hotel near the port, for a restful night before embarking or after disembarking, the railway station to enable passengers to travel between London – it was nearly always London – and the ship.

But possibly the most significant difference between ports in the 1980s and ports in the 1930s is the shift from rail to road transport. This is at its most obvious at the Channel ports, where getting cars and lorries on and off ships constitutes the major part of the business today at places like Dover and Folkestone, and where nearly everything came and went by rail before the Second World War. The appearance of these ports from the air is consequently strikingly different now from what it was before the car-ferries took over the traffic.

But a similar change is noticeable at the non-ferry ports, where photographs show lorries taking a very poor second place to freight trains even as late as the 1950s and the situation completely reversed today. There are some very thriving ports now, of course – Felixstowe and Shoreham are good examples – which have developed entirely on the basis of road transport, and where the railway has never been of any importance at all.

Southampton, Hampshire: the dock area

Southampton was developed by the Normans at the point where two rivers, the Test and the Itchen, meet. The walled town which grew up there had a considerable trade with France and the Mediterranean, the principal exports being wool and cloth, and the imports mainly wine and various luxury goods. Ships were first loaded and unloaded over hards (gently sloping banks, made firm with stone and gravel), but later by means of wooden jetties, and finally at one of the three quays built out over the mud banks, the West Quay, the Watergate Quay and the Castle Quay. The subsequent spread of the town and the port across the former mudflats has left these medieval quays, like the town wall itself, high and dry and a considerable distance from today's waterfront. The southern frontage of the old town of Southampton, the Town Quay area, is still close to the river. The continuation of a road along Town Quay, which follows the original shoreline further east, constructed after the Victorian engineers had pushed back the sea, is appropriately called Canute Road.

The port's prosperity declined during the seventeenth and eighteenth centuries and the situation began to improve only with the arrival of the railway in 1840. Just before that, the construction of the Royal Victoria Pier in 1833, allowed ships to the Isle of Wight and Southampton to operate at any state of the tide. The new Eastern Docks were opened in 1842. They were used until 1960, when the services were suspended, by passenger ships linking Southampton with Le Havre and the Channel Islands, and also for a while by the Royal Mail and P & O liners. The Outer Dock was completed in 1840 and the only impounded dock in the port, the Inner Dock, in 1851. During the 1939–45 War the Inner Dock lost most of its warehouses in air raids and was eventually filled in to provide space for new dock buildings. The large Empress Dock was opened in 1890 to accommodate the much bigger ships which had come into service by that time. Since then the development of the port has been more or less continuous, especially towards the west, with more and more of the mud banks being reclaimed to provide the necessary land.

The Ocean Dock, then known as the White Star Dock, was built shortly before the First World War, in 1911, mainly to handle the very profitable and prestigious transatlantic traffic. The Ocean Terminal alongside the Ocean Dock was opened in 1950. The venture was ill-judged and the building had a very short life. By 1960 passengers travelling to and from America had transferred their custom to the airlines and the Terminal, the biggest in the world, was demolished in 1983.

This long period of growth, decay and change is clearly shown in photograph **64**, taken in 1981 and looking north-west. The Empress Dock is at right centre. The Ocean Terminal is the long building running diagonally across the centre of the picture, with the Empress Dock to the right of it and the Ocean Dock to the left. The large warehousing, parking and movement area to the south of the Ocean Terminal and the Empress Dock occupies wholly made-up ground. The original shoreline ran westward in front of the trees at top centre and as far as the L-shaped Town Quay, at top left. At that point it swung sharply north, past the church and two multi-storey office blocks, centre top. Royal Pier, the first of Southampton's nineteenth-century port installations, lies just to the north of Town Quay.

To the right of the belt of trees, marking Queen's Park, at top centre, and partly masked by the trees, is one of Southampton's most impressive port monuments, the former South-Western Hotel. It adjoined the Terminus railway station, the tracks to which ran north-east, to the left of the tall white tower-block in the right-hand top corner of the picture. Built in two stages, the first in 1872 and the second in the first decade of the

64 Southampton, Hampshire: Empress Dock, Ocean Dock and Ocean Terminal. Cambridge University Collection, CNY 32: February 1981.

present century, this large hotel was intended to serve the overnight needs of passengers to and from America, South Africa and the Far East, and of their friends who came to meet them or to see them off. It was requisitioned by the Government during the Second World War and now, as South-Western House, is used for office purposes and by the BBC.

Photograph **65**, taken in 1948, shows part of the port area as it was in the immediate post-war years. The River Itchen flows diagonally across the top of the picture. The Empress Dock is in the centre of the photograph, with Princess Alexandra Dock beyond it to the north, on the river side.

The Inner Dock, to the left of the Princess Alexandra, has not yet been filled in, but one can easily see that it was quite unsuited to all but the smallest ships.

Perhaps the most interesting feature of this photograph, however, is the view it provides of the Ocean Terminal under construction, between the Empress and Ocean Docks. The steel frame is in the process of erection and the piled foundations for the remainder of the building are clearly visible.

An interesting comparison with **65** is provided by **66**, taken much earlier, in 1927. Nearly all the dockside sheds shown in this picture were de-

65 Southampton: general view of dock area. Cambridge University Collection, AQ 84: June 1948.

stroyed by bombing during the Second World War. The site of the future Ocean Terminal is indicated by a long double row of sheds. The large four-funnelled ship, the 'Berengaria', in the top left-hand corner is in the Trafalgar graving dock, which came into operation in 1905 and has since been filled in, as has the Prince of Wales Dock (1895), leading off the Empress Dock, seen, with a ship in it, just right of centre in this photograph.

Liverpool docks, Merseyside

The first dock to be built in Liverpool, the Old Dock, was completed in 1715, on the site of what is now Canning Place, south of the Pier Head and well inland from the present Canning Dock, which was originally a tidal basin leading to the Old Dock. Until the 1820s, all dock development

was to the south. The first extension of the dock area northwards was in 1821, when the new Princes Dock was opened. Before this, none of the Liverpool docks had been protected by security walls against theft and damage. Jesse Hartley, who was Dock Engineer from 1824 to 1860, was responsible for building a great wall all along the dock area, separating it from the city, with gates which slid into slots in the walls and a railway running just inside the wall. Hartley's Albert Dock, of 1844–5, embodied a new conception of dock design, with an enclosed dock surrounded by warehouses on all sides. With this system, and with the additional safeguard of the continuous dock wall, security was as good as could be effected.

During the present century Liverpool suffered a series of major blows, so far as its docks were concerned. The first was the decision of the

66 Southampton: earlier view of dock area. Southampton Reference Library: 1927.

White Star Line, in 1907, to transfer its North Atlantic express passenger service to Southampton. The Cunard Line followed suit in 1919. Damage to the warehouses and other port installations from air raids during the Second World War was very heavy, but perhaps the most crippling blow of all was the introduction of container ships during the 1960s. The existing Liverpool docks had no space for receiving and stacking containers and, as a result, trade at the port declined seriously, a situation which has only recently begun to improve with the construction of the Royal Seaforth container terminal, much further to the north.

The history and characteristics of the Port of Liverpool are well illustrated by the three aerial photographs which are included here.

Photograph **67** shows the oldest section of the docks. The Landing Stage and Pier Head are at bottom centre. Immediately behind these can be seen the Royal Liver Building, on the left, and

next to it the Cunard Building. Continuing along the waterfront towards the right one comes to the great square complex of the Albert Dock (1844–45) and between here and the road the Canning Dock and the larger Salthouse Dock, completed in 1753 and reconstructed in 1845. Canning Place is opposite the storage area between Canning and Salthouse Docks. To the left of the Landing Stage is Princes Dock. The dock wall is on the nearer side of the main road which crosses the picture.

The Albert, Canning and Salthouse Docks are silted up and no longer in use. Princes Dock is still usable but, as the photograph makes clear, it is of no commercial importance. Only very small craft are moored there.

Nine pre-Second World War docks can be seen in **68**. All are approached through a lock system which makes them independent of tidal fluctuations. The entrances from the Mersey are on the extreme left and right of the picture. Reading from left to right, the docks are first the Brockle-

67 Liverpool docks, Merseyside: oldest section. Cambridge University Collection, RC8–FM 190: September 1983. Scale 1:13,250.

bank, then the Canada, with its three branch docks and its graving dock between No. 1 and No. 2 branch docks. This dock was quite busy at the time when the photograph was taken, with two ships loading or unloading and a third in the graving dock. South of this is the Huskisson, with two branch docks, four ships berthed and considerable warehousing space. Below this are the Sandon and Wellington Docks and lastly, on the bottom edge of the picture, the Bramley Moore Dock. In none of the last three does there appear to be any activity at all.

The general impression which one gains from this photograph is of a somewhat struggling port,

making a modest living by dealing with general cargo vessels. The built-up area to the right of the road running down the centre of the picture and dividing the docks from the town is obviously a permanent barrier to any attempt to develop this part of the Port of Liverpool for container traffic. The storage space required simply is not there. For this group of docks, it is clearly general cargo or nothing and, to cater for this, the capacity would seem excessive. Closures would appear to be inevitable.

Photograph **69**, however, tells a very different story. The Seaforth Container Port is on the left and, to the right of it, the Gladstone and Hornby

68 Liverpool docks. Cambridge University Collection, RC8–FM 185: September 1983. Scale 1:11,300.

Docks, with the Customs Offices occupying much of the broad island between the Gladstone and Hornby Docks. Within the Gladstone and Hornby area, there is not a great deal of activity, with only two ships berthed and the graving dock empty.

In the Container Port to the left, however, the situation is more encouraging. It is difficult to imagine a photograph which would better illustrate the contrast between the old shipping world and the new. The new port has been designed specifically for the container trade. There are enormous stacking areas to the west and south of the dock and the dock itself has been planned to give big container ships plenty of room to manœuvre. Equally important, there is good access to the motorway system. The twin-track road, Princess Way, which goes off the top of the picture from the two-level junction leads directly and quickly to the M 57 and M 58. The Container

69 Liverpool docks: the Seaforth Container Port. Cambridge University Collection, RC8–FM 181: September 1983. Scale 1:11,300.

Port has assumed from the beginning that its cargoes will arrive and leave by road. The older docks relied on the railway to move their freight to and from the ships. The Seaforth Port does not have railway sidings.

A further and important difference between the traditional type of dock and the Seaforth type is emphasised by the dock wall, which ends at the Gladstone Dock. Throughout the eighteenth and nineteenth centuries and for most of the twentieth, cargo, brought in and unloaded in separate small units, was relatively easy to steal. The wall was there to prevent this from happening. Containers, however, are large, heavy and extremely difficult to steal, at least within the port area. When one is stolen, which is rarely, the method is usually to hijack the lorry transporting it to or from the dock and this, of course, is not the responsibility of the port authorities. So Seaforth has a fence and gates, like any other kind of industrial property, but no wall. Nobody is going to climb over the fence and disappear with a container on his shoulder; but, without the dockyard wall, a good many lengths of timber or sacks of grain would have disappeared without a trace.

London docks

The Port of London officially extends for 150 km along both banks of the Thames eastwards from Teddington. Within this area there were, fifty years ago, 280 ha of enclosed docks. They were dug out during the eighteenth and nineteenth centuries and they are being filled in during the twentieth, as bigger ships and containerisation have forced sea-going traffic further downstream towards the estuary.

At its peak, the London dock system (see Fig. 4) comprised, running from Tower Bridge and towards Woolwich, the St Katharine Dock (1829); London Dock (1805); Surrey Commercial Docks, built in stages during the 1870s; Regent's Canal Dock (1815); West India Dock (1880); and King George V Dock (1921). Surrounding each dock complex were the houses where the dock-workers lived. The whole area was known as Dockland and it had a very marked character and cohesion of its own. The close intermingling of the docks with the community brought problems as well as advantages. On the one hand, the dockers had to travel only a short distance to their work, but on the other, security was appallingly difficult. Even with an intricate system of gates and high walls, the constant movement of people and vehicles in and out of the docks made thieving almost impossible to prevent. The inhabitants of London's dockland were a remarkable mixture of the hard-working, highly respectable working class and a substantial criminal element, much of it foreign. It is worth noting, perhaps, that the walls protecting the docks are immensely impressive when one stands by them on the ground, but fall into insignificance from the air. One observes the same in the case of prisons.

The combination of a winding river, congested buildings and dock security measures meant that, until aerial photography revealed the area as a whole for the first time, it was impossible to obtain a satisfactory overall impression of the London docks. Even those who had spent a lifetime working in them had no real idea of how extensive the docks were and what a great acreage of water had been enclosed.

During the nineteenth century, the various docks developed a high degree of specialisation. Tilbury concerned itself mainly with ships sailing to and from Asia and Australia, the Victoria and the Albert Docks concentrated on grain, tobacco and frozen meat – the cold stores for frozen meat here were the largest in the world – and in the West India Dock the principal cargoes were tropical hardwoods, grain and seed, sugar and rum. Millwall was mainly a grain dock, the Surrey Commercial handled imports of timber, grain, bacon and cheese, and the London and St Katharine specialised in wool, tea, wine and spirits, and rubber.

Both the dock installations and the dockers' houses suffered great damage during the Second World War, and this accelerated the inevitable decay of what had, until 1939, been Britain's greatest port. Half the storage capacity of the docks was destroyed and much of it was never rebuilt. The whole dock area west of Tilbury now, from a shipping point of view, displays very little activity.

The East India Dock, once the home of the tea clippers, was the first to close completely, in 1947. This dock had an Import and Export section. The Import Dock was dried out during the 1939–45 war and used for the construction of caissons for the invasion harbours on the Normandy coast. Soon after the war, the Export Dock was filled in and Brunswick Wharf Power Station built on the site. The London and St Katharine Docks followed, in 1968–69, and the Surrey Commercial Docks in 1970. The whole area is now in the process of redevelopment, with warehousing, hotels, offices, flats and houses gradually taking the place of loading and unloading ships. Dockland is showing strong signs of becoming fashionable, with the middle classes steadily taking over an area which half a century ago was almost exclusively working-class.

The photographs show parts of the London docks as they appeared in 1972. Photograph **70** looks west-north-west up the Thames, from a point over the southern end of the Surrey Docks. The Surrey Docks have ceased to operate and, as one can see in the bottom right-hand corner, they are already being filled in. Many of the sheds in the bottom half of the picture were destroyed by wartime bombing and the sites subsequently cleared. Their outline appears on the photograph as a grid of foundations, the ghosts of a once busy area.

The London Dock, extending across the top right area of the picture, has not yet been filled in, but there are no ships in any of the basins. St Katharine Dock, to the right of Tower Bridge, is

70 London docks, looking WNW up the Thames. Cambridge University Collection, BIJ 96: May 1972.

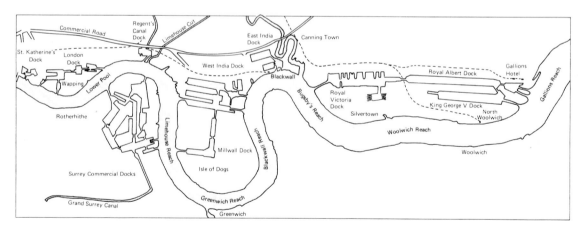

Fig. 4 The London docks.

71 London docks, looking WNW over the Isle of Dogs. Cambridge University Collection, BIJ 76: May 1972.

by now functioning as a marine and trade centre. Almost the only ships to be seen on the river by this time are barges.

Photographs **71** and **72** show the docks two or three kilometres down river from the previous photograph. There is less of a scene of desolation here, although the area is far from busy.

In **71**, the stretch of the Thames at the bottom of the picture is Blackwall Reach. The three docks occupying the centre of the photograph are those of the West India Dock, with Blackwall Basin and Poplar Dock just below them and to the right. One end of the Millwall Dock can be seen on the left, and across Limehouse Reach and on another bend of the river are the Surrey Docks. The Regent's Canal Dock is the small area of water to the right of this bend.

Poplar High Street runs parallel to the north section of the West India Dock, between the blocks of multi-storey flats, and the Blackwall Tunnel goes under the river just to the left of the oil storage tanks.

Photograph **72**, taken from a point over Green-

wich Reach, shows another panorama of idle cranes. The main section of the West India Docks is on the right and linked to it and running at right angles is Millwall Inner Dock, partly marked in the photograph by the long range of modern warehouses, built to replace those destroyed by wartime bombing. Millwall Outer Dock is at left centre, and immediately facing it across the river are the South and Greenland Docks of the Surrey Commercial Docks complex. Millwall Park is the large open space below Millwall Outer Dock. The block of flats on both sides of the Inner Dock were built during the 1950s and 1960s, to replace dwellings lost during bombing and as part of a slum clearance programme.

Two general features of these three photographs of the Port of London are perhaps particularly striking. The first involves a certain, but worthwhile effort of the imagination. When seen from the air, these docks resemble a series of lakes spread out between Tower Bridge and North Woolwich. They are lakes of a considerable size. The London Docks basin alone, for

87

72 London docks, from a point over Greenwich Reach. Cambridge University Collection, BII 74: May 1972.

example, is 238 m long and 137 m wide, and the water area of the Millwall Docks is 21 ha. These docks were dug out by pick-and-shovel labour and, in the case of the earlier docks, the earth was taken away by horses and carts. Immense numbers of men were employed and they worked fast. St Katharine Dock, for example, employed 2,500 men for two years. It would be something of an exaggeration to compare the construction of the London docks to the building of the Pyramids, but it should, even so, be difficult to look at aerial photographs of these enormous engineering achievements without thinking of the vast expenditure of human energy which produced them.

The second aspect of the Port of London photographs which seems deserving of special comment is that railway facilities are practically non-existent. There is no network of sidings to serve the docks and there never has been. The contrast with other large British ports is very marked. There are three reasons for this. The first is the River Thames and the canals linked to it. Bulky cargoes could be transferred to barges or lighters and moved by water from ocean-going ships to their final destinations. The second is the size and importance of London itself. A high proportion of the customers for goods arriving by sea at the Port of London were in London. Even in the days of horse-drawn transport, the factory, flour-mill or wholesaler for whom the goods were destined was very likely to be only a few kilometres from the docks. Railway transport was of no advantage to them. And the third reason for the absence of railways lay in the nature of many of the commodities which the port handled. For such things as wines and spirits, tobacco, tea and coffee – goods of high value and small bulk – their first home after leaving the dock was either a bonded store outside the dock, or a specialist warehouse not very far away. Once again, the railway was irrelevant.

88

73 Cardiff docks, South Glamorgan. Cambridge University Collection, cz 60: June 1949.

Cardiff docks, South Glamorgan

Throughout the nineteenth century there was great competition[1] between the South Wales ports – Swansea, Newport, Cardiff and Neath – for the coal trade. A rapid turn-round of ships was all-important, and the attempt to achieve this more successfully than one's rivals was the main reason for the harbour and dock improvements in the first half of the century. By 1820 Newport had become the most important coal port in South Wales, but heavy investment in dock facilities enabled Cardiff to catch up fifty years later. The coming of steamships brought a big increase in shipments of steam coal, especially of the smoke-less variety, which was mostly exported through Cardiff.

But coal exports were only part of the story and, for many years, the smallest part. In the eighteenth century, iron-smelting and iron-forging were of prime importance. The iron industry was the dominant element in the economy of South Wales, with a heavy investment of capital and a number of production units which were among the largest in Britain. Tinplate manufacturing was established in South Wales in the 1740s and, like iron and steel, it had a large export trade for nearly two hundred years. Copper-smelting, too, was on a large scale. Between 1800 and 1840, nearly ninety per cent of Britain's copper was produced in South Wales, a high proportion of it from imported ores. One tonne of pure copper took three tonnes of coal to produce, so it was obviously cheaper to bring the ore to the coal, rather than the coal to the ore. There was an added advantage, in that ships which brought copper ore from Cornwall, Anglesey and Ireland were able to return with coal.

The coal seams in South Wales run mostly north and south, towards the coast, and so first the canals and then the railways were able to use the valleys in order to bring coal, iron and other products down to the ports. Cardiff had the benefit of the Glamorganshire Canal from 1794 onwards and the railways from the 1840s. The canal was closed to traffic in 1942 and the section

74 Cardiff docks. Cambridge University Collection, CZ 56: June 1949.

running through the town and towards the docks was filled in soon afterwards. The canal was not unimportant – the products of the Merthyr Tydfil ironworks reached Cardiff this way for many years – but without the dense network of railways with which South Wales was equipped by the 1860s the enormous industrial development of later Victorian times would have been impossible.

Two 1949 photographs, **73** and **74**, show the legacy of this development. In **73**, Roath Basin, leading into Roath Dock, is on the right-hand side of the photograph. The Basin was opened in 1874 and the Dock in 1887. Parallel to them to the right, but just off the picture, is the Queen Alexandra Dock (1907). These are still operational, but the elaborate apparatus of traverser coal-hoists, belt conveyors and other loading and unloading equipment was cleared away during the 1950s and 1960s, after the overseas export trade in coal had almost disappeared. When ships moved from coal to oil fuelling, Cardiff, like a number of other places in Britain, ceased to be a coal port. In 1949, however, many of these

installations were still in place, and they can be seen in the top right corner of the picture, along the right-hand side of the Roath Dock, behind the two berthed ships. The railway bringing the coal enters the picture at the top left, between the two housing estates, and curves down towards the dock at the point where it reaches the coast, behind the large, light-coloured flour mill. A number of branch lines then fan out left, towards the ironworks, and the main line continues parallel to the long side of the dock. A series of sidings then drops away from it to the dock, like ribs from the spine. Coal trucks were unloaded at the dock end of the sidings and the coal was moved to the coal-hoists by conveyor and then into the ships. Several of the hoists can be distinguished along the quayside behind the ships. There are others, with their conveyors, on the right-hand side of the Roath Basin and more on both sides of Bute East Dock, the broad expanse of water which crosses the left-hand side of the picture in a gentle curve.

Bute East Dock was opened in 1859. It is no

90

75 Grimsby docks, Humberside. Photair Ltd., Eccles, 2650: late 1940s. Now in the Cambridge University Collection.

longer in use for shipping, but serves as a reservoir for the iron and steel works. Bute West Dock (1839), which runs parallel to the East Dock and below it was filled in during 1972. Its basin and some of the buildings surrounding it have been adapted for the use of the Welsh Industrial and Maritime Museum.

Below the entrance to the Roath Basin one can see Cardiff's Pierhead and Landing Stage, and below them in turn the first of the Mountstuart Dry Docks.

Photograph **74** continues the pattern of Cardiff docks towards the Bristol Channel, with the big Queen Alexandra Dock on the right and the Roath Dock on the left. The basin below the Queen Alexandra Dock has since been filled in. This picture shows very clearly the elaborate railway and conveyor system used throughout the port for loading coal. At the time the photograph was taken, the system was still operational and lines of coal trucks are visible on both the inclines and the sidings.

What remains of Cardiff's docks is an evocative memorial to the great days of coal and iron, which brought the port into being and gave it, for a century, international importance. Once the international trade in coal had gone, the decline of the docks was inevitable.

One can obtain an excellent impression of how the coal-hoist system worked by studying a very high-quality aerial photograph of Grimsby docks **(75)**, which was probably taken in the late 1940s, though the type of ship shown would have suggested a date quite twenty years earlier. The contents of the coal trucks were tipped into underground hoppers situated on the left of the road and then taken up the covered conveyor to the hoist, from which it was discharged directly into the holds of the small coastal vessels waiting below. There were variants to the system, according to the layout of the dock, the type of vessel to be loaded and the surrounding terrain, but what took place at Grimsby was basically similar to the Cardiff method.

Reference

1. See A.H. John, *The Industrial Development of South Wales*, 1950, pp. 116–17.

Railways

The history of railways in Britain can be divided into two stages. In the first, up till about 1830, trucks were hauled over rails by horses, or in some instances moved by gravity, and in the second, from the 1830s onwards, they were hauled by locomotives. Aerial photography is of great value in locating and recording the abandoned routes of both types of railway and in showing how they were related to the places they were built to serve.

The British railway network – that is, for freight and passenger trains hauled by locomotives – was at its maximum size in the early 1930s. From then onwards, a steady process of closure has reduced it to about two-thirds of what it once was. When a line is completely closed, the normal procedure is to lift its track, use the rails elsewhere or sell them for scrap and to demolish all iron or steel bridges and viaducts, which have a high scrap value. Masonry bridges are usually left until they show signs of becoming dangerous or unless they happen to interfere with road widening or realignment. Cuttings are often used by local authorities as rubbish dumps and, where embankments form part of the land sold to farmers, they will probably be levelled in due course, as will the raised track-bed of a railway which ran across high ground. Signal boxes will be pulled down, station buildings sold off for conversion to housing or workshops. In urban areas, where the land is valuable, buildings of one kind or another are almost certain to be erected on any flat land, including the line of the track, which once belonged to the railway.

In these various ways, it is possible within twenty years virtually to erase a railway, in the sense that from the ground one can discover very few traces of where it used to run. But, seen from the air, a railway does not disappear so completely. One can plot its course by mentally linking the clues which still remain along its route, the not quite overgrown strip through woodland, the little bridges and the cuttings which no-one has yet bothered about, the tunnel entrances, the little coal-yards which no longer serve any purpose, the areas formerly covered by sidings which have not yet found a buyer.

But there are three particular fields in which aerial photography really comes into its own as a tool for documenting the history of railways. The first concerns tunnels, the second railway terminals and the third railway workshops.

The construction of a big railway tunnel was a major engineering feat, especially with the equipment and materials available during the first half of the nineteenth century, when most of our tunnels were built. If the tunnel burrowed through a mountain, as it not infrequently had to, the excavated material had to be removed through both ends of the tunnel, as work proceeded. There was no other way. But if it went under downland or if it had to be a tunnel because a cutting would have been too deep for safety, then it was possible to drive shafts downwards along its route, partly for the removal of rock and earth and partly to act as permanent smoke-vents afterwards. From the air, one can follow the course of the tunnel in this way, with the brick chimney vents and the mounds of excavated soil, now grassed over and often with trees on them, following one another like a string of beads, monuments to prodigious hard labour.

One can appreciate that, say, Victoria or Paddington stations are big, simply by walking about inside them and using them, but nothing but an aerial photograph really conveys the extent of the ground which they and their approach tracks occupy. Bought cheaply enough last century, these huge sites are now worth many millions of pounds and, if British Rail no longer required them, their sale would probably cause some disruption of the property market, as well as providing exceptional opportunities for imaginative town planning. But, with the advantages of an aerial perspective, one can have other thoughts. One can, for example, observe the concentration of railway resources which has already taken place in Leeds, Cheltenham, Glasgow and Manchester, and one can marvel at the absurdity of having three mainline termini, Euston, St Pancras and King's Cross, strung out along the Euston Road within half a mile of one another, a situation which made sense in the days of separate and competing Victorian railway companies, but

76 **Railway construction near Charwelton, Northamptonshire.** Cambridge University Collection, BSD 57: March 1975.

which is ridiculous today. And, with this same vast estate of railway land, one can see the huge area occupied until the Second World War, when air raids put a somewhat premature end to its career, by the railway's Somerstown coal and potato depot, which supplied Londoners with a large proportion of their requirements of these two commodities for more than a century, and on the site of which the new British Library is slowly rising.

The third natural subject for aerial photography where railways are concerned is the railway workshops, more particularly those at Crewe and Swindon. Up to twenty-five years ago, these were great kingdoms in their own right. The workshops at Crewe and Swindon each covered more than 200 ha and employed thousands of people, building, repairing and overhauling whatever their respective railways required in the way of locomotives and rolling-stock. Suddenly, in the

93

1960s, British Rail, forced to rationalise and economise, discovered that the workshops which had been considered as eternal and essential as the Bank of England were no longer necessary and that most of their work could be carried out more cheaply by private firms. Demolition began immediately and a large part of Crewe is now a desert as a result. At Swindon, where the railway workshops were almost as big as at Crewe, there has been much greater success in finding new uses for the site of the works and those who knew this part of the town in the early 1960s would find it almost unrecognisable today. Before-and-after aerial photographs provide an unequalled understanding of what has taken place.

Railway construction near Charwelton, Northamptonshire

'The engineering of the early railways', Terry Coleman comments,[1] 'was like nothing before. Only the canals of the eighteenth century can compare in any way to the railways that so soon killed them. Only the cathedrals were so vast in idea: nothing before was so vast in scale.' He goes on to say that 'there is hardly a branch line in Britain whose earthworks would not be marvelled at if they were those of a new road or an ancient fort'. This is no exaggeration. The railways could not climb anything more than gentle slopes, and in order to provide the gradients required enormous quantities of earth and rock had to be shifted, to construct the necessary tunnels, cuttings and embankments. The work was all done by navvies, who loaded the trucks, and by horses who pulled them along temporary rail-tracks. Each man shovelled twenty tonnes of material into trucks every day.

The contractors were working against the clock and each section of the work had to be completed in the shortest possible time. This meant, among other things, that it was important not to move excavated material any further than was absolutely necessary. The usual method of achieving this was to construct embankments with what was taken out of tunnels and cuttings, the cut-and-fill technique. This was not always possible, however, and sometimes it was necessary to buy additional land on one or both sides of the track, either for dumping purposes or for excavating material with which to form an embankment.

Photograph **76** shows such a site. It is near Charwelton, in Northamptonshire, on the line from Aylesbury to Rugby, which was abandoned in the 1960s as part of the Beeching cuts. The material, which is of a chalky nature, almost certainly came from the tunnel which began just north of Charwelton. It would have been brought along a horse-hauled light railway from the tunnel entrance, the temporary rails being moved away from the main route of the railway, towards the left of the picture, as the work proceeded. In the course of time, possibly quite soon, the spoil slipped sideways down the incline, to finish in its present position. One presumes this was allowed for and that tipping was stopped while there was still a safety margin. Had it continued, the river running by the side of the woodland on the left-hand side of the picture would ultimately have been blocked.

The site was well chosen, because the presence of such great quantities of material by the side of the embankment carrying the railway track prevented the embankment itself from slipping away down the steep slope adjoining it.

Reference

1. *The Railway Navvies*, 1965, p. 33.

The railway complex at Leeds, West Yorkshire

The ingenuity and the engineering achievement of a complicated road or rail system cannot be properly understood or appreciated on the ground, particularly if, as is often the case, it happens to be in a heavily built-up area.

Leeds provides just such an example. Photograph **77** was taken in 1959, at a time when four things which were to be of great significance to both the city and the region had not yet happened – the Beeching Plan, which was to greatly change the pattern of Britain's railways, had not yet appeared; the network of motorways was still a long way from Leeds; the textile industry had not yet begun to suffer from the recession which was to cause it to shrink to a quarter of its former size; and Leeds still had no air connections worth talking about with London. In these circumstances Leeds Railway Station was the transport centre of the city. It was busy, it was prosperous, and it had prestige.

That prestige was emphasised by the building of the Queen's Hotel, adjoining the station. It was opened in 1935 and it has quite rightly been scheduled as a national monument of archaeological and historical importance, although its glory has faded together with that of the railway station. What is fairly unmistakably the station can be seen towards the top right-hand corner of

77 The railway complex at Leeds, West Yorkshire. Cambridge University Collection, ZY 3: July 1959.

the picture. The Queen's Hotel is the modern E-shaped flat-roofed building a short distance to the left of it.

Since this photograph was taken, great changes have taken place at Leeds City Station. To raise money, a new entrance building, combined with shops and offices, has been constructed between the Queen's Hotel and the train shed. The former booking-office block, linking the station with the hotel, has been abandoned and the adjacent section of the train shed has been turned into a car park. Twenty-five years after the photograph was taken, Leeds City is only a shadow of its former grand self.

But the pattern of lines leading in and out of the station remains. To the right of the platforms and running off the picture at the top right is the line to York and Hull, the only line to go through the station. The Wakefield line is the high-level one which disappears off the picture at bottom centre, and curving away under it, towards the right, is the Sheffield and Goole line. The line to Carlisle goes off at the left, with branches to Huddersfield

and Bradford not long after leaving the station. All these lines still combine to make Leeds one of the most important railway centres in the north of England.

The photograph illustrates a number of other aspects of industrial history, in addition to that which is concerned primarily with the railway. The docks linked to the River Aire and the Leeds and Liverpool Canal run up towards the station, on the left-hand side of the tracks. The canal is clearly visible just to the near side of the docks. The junction of the docks with the River Aire is near the centre of the left-hand edge of the photograph, but the river itself, running diagonally across the centre, on the right of the Goods Station, is concealed by buildings at this point. The river is taken underground below the railway and emerges below the viaduct at the bottom end of the station platforms. The canal terminates at the rail tracks.

The Goods Station, the group of single-storeyed, dark-coloured buildings to the left of the factories bordering the docks, was demolished during

95

78 Swindon, Wiltshire: the railway area. Cambridge University Collection, RC8–ER 125: July 1982. Scale 1:13,400.

the 1970s. Though it was once a key factor in the city's economy, there was no longer the freight to justify its continued existence.

One of the saddest events in the recent history of Leeds is illustrated in the top right-hand corner of the picture. This great circular block is Quarry Hill Flats. Completed in 1940, it was demolished in 1975, after having been so badly vandalised by its tenants that it was no longer habitable. The aerial photograph shows how Quarry Hill was planned: a tall outer ring, with free-standing tower blocks within the open courtyard. Claimed at the time they were built to be the best working-class flats in Europe, they proved to be a disaster.

Working-class people in Leeds had no wish to live in flats.

The railway workshops at Swindon, Wiltshire

In 1840 Swindon was chosen by the Great Western Railway's Locomotive Superintendent as 'our principal engine establishment'. It soon became an important junction for the lines to Gloucester, Cheltenham, Bristol and South Wales, as well as a major workshop centre and locomotive depot. Once it had been selected as the Great Western's

79 Swindon: the railway workshops in 1849. Detail from a water-colour drawing, Swindon Public Library.

main base for building and repairing rolling stock and locomotives, it became necessary to build a new town, where the men and their families could live, since the old market town of Swindon, 1.5 km away up on the hill, was unsuitable for development. During the 1840s and 1850s, a new railway village was therefore laid out in the fields, close to the railway station and the workshops. These elegant little terraces still survive, surrounded by acres of subsequent speculative building of much inferior architectural merit.

The workshops began to produce locomotives in 1846 and within a few years they were employing nearly 2,000 men. By 1900 Swindon railway works as a whole provided a living for 10,000 people. The works, together with their sidings, eventually came to cover approximately 100 ha. From the 1960s onwards, however, there has been contraction on a scale which would at one time have been considered impossible. The whole of the carriage, waggon and locomotive building section of the works has been closed down and only repair and maintenance work is now carried out at Swindon. Most of the workshops have been demolished.

Photograph **78** shows the railway area of Swindon after the contraction and demolition had taken place. North is to the top: the main line to London and Bristol cuts across the bottom half of the picture from right to left; the Gloucester and Cheltenham line branches off it and runs up the centre of the photograph. At its peak, the railway workshops occupied about a quarter of the area shown in this photograph. Most of the workshops were to the north of the Bristol–London line, but there was a narrow belt of them along the south side. As a rough guide, one can say that everything to the north of the Bristol–London tracks which lies below the two large housing estates was once occupied by railway workshops and their associated sidings. The section to the right of the Cheltenham–Swindon line is now almost entirely used for other purposes and so, too, is the former railway property to the south of the Bristol–London line.

Much of the territory within the bottom non-

80 Swindon: the railway village in 1849. Detail from a water-colour drawing, Swindon Public Library.

housing area enclosed by the two railway lines on the right of the picture is now occupied by Swindon College of Further Education. The carriage and waggon works of the railway were formerly here and these workshops were totally demolished and cleared during the 1960s and early 1970s. Of the buildings still used by the railway, the carriage repair shops are to the left of the Cheltenham line and immediately adjoining it. The shops for maintaining and overhauling locomotives are on the left of the carriage shops, and further left still, towards the left-hand edge of the picture, below the playing field, is the range of sidings which are mostly occupied nowadays by superannuated diesel locomotives in the process of being dismantled for scrap.

The municipal sewage disposal plant takes up most of the top left-hand corner, while to the right of it, on the other side of the railway line, one can see part of an estate of new factories, built as part of the town's successful programme to broaden the local industrial base and to transform it from a community almost entirely dependent on the railway to one better suited to the present age. Most of the hundreds of houses shown in this picture were, as recently as twenty years ago, lived in by big families whose income came from the railway. Nowadays very few of them have any connection with the railway.

The bottom third of the photograph, south of the railway tracks, is full of interesting features. The narrow area bordering the tracks between the right-hand edge of the picture and the park in the centre was, until the 1960s, completely covered by railway workshops. Most of these have been demolished and the sites are now used for car-parking. The surviving workshop buildings, at right angles to the railway, are now let to individual firms, as small factories and warehouses.

Below these converted workshops and to the right of the park are the six streets of houses, in

81 Swindon: a row of houses in the railway village. Photograph, Borough of Thamesdown.

two groups of three, which formed the original railway village. At the top of the piazza separating the two groups is the large building which was designed, and for three-quarters of a century used, as a Mechanics' Institute.

Swindon Public Library possesses a remarkable bird's-eye view of New Swindon, the railway village, made in 1849. It is a water-colour drawing and complements modern aerial photographs in a most interesting way. Photographs **79** and **80** are enlargements of two parts of it, the railway workshops and the railway village. Photograph **81** shows a row of houses in the railway village after modernisation; **82** shows the railway village as it was in the mid-1960s before modernisation, while **83** shows the same section of the village after modernisation in the 1970s.

An aerial photograph puts the village into its context and reveals its shape and pattern, complementing the kind of detail which is obtained perfectly satisfactorily from the ground.

It might usefully be mentioned in passing that until the railway workshops entered their period of decline in the 1960s, they were characterised by very strict discipline and security. A high stone wall, known locally as The Wall, surrounded the whole of the workshop area and employees went in and out by means of two tunnels leading underneath the tracks. There was a checkpoint at the entrance to each tunnel. The entrances were in the wall which ran along the north side of the railway village.

An abandoned Scottish railway, near Darvel, Strathclyde

Until 1939 it was possible to travel by train both east and west from Darvel: west towards Kilmarnock and east in the direction of Hamilton and Motherwell. In the 1920s this part of Scotland had a wonderfully intricate and convenient system of

82 Swindon: the railway village before modernisation. Photograph, Borough of Thamesdown: mid-1960s.

83 Swindon: the same section of the railway village, after modernisation in the 1970s. Photograph, Ann Nicholls.

100

84 An abandoned Scottish railway, near Darvel, Strathclyde. Cambridge University Collection, AMB 69: August 1965.

railways. It was cut back severely in the 1930s and then again following the Beeching Report of 1963. Darvel lost its railway in two stages, west to Gatehead in 1939 and east to Strathaven in 1964.

The stretch shown in **84** formed part of the eastern section, that is, it had been out of use for twenty-six years when the photograph was taken, in 1965. It illustrates the normal British Rail policy of demolishing iron and steel bridges, in order to recoup the scrap value of the metal, but allowing masonry viaducts to remain, unless they should happen to be in the way of road development or of some other form of construction requiring the site.

In the top right-hand corner the small bridge still standing, used only for farm purposes, is of stone or brick. It has been there since the railway was built, as a condition of taking the line along this particular route, since without it the farmer would have been unable to move stock and vehicles between fields on either side of the line. This con-

sideration did not apply to the bridge closer to the centre of the picture, since its purpose was only to take the railway across the road. Once the railway had been closed, the bridge had no function, so the girders were removed and sold and the supporting piers left in position.

The masonry viaduct does, however, present British Rail with a problem, or could conceivably do so at some time in the future. When a rural railway ceases to operate, the land through which it runs is normally offered for sale to the farmer whose territory it adjoins. Sometimes the offer is accepted, sometimes not, but after the usual haggling excellent bargains are often obtainable and, once the land is sold, the new owner is, of course, free to carry out whatever levelling work he pleases. He may or may not feel it is worth the expense involved.

A viaduct, such as the one shown in the photograph, is quite another matter, however. No matter who owns it, to demolish it costs a lot of money and to allow it to stand without main-

101

85 The route of a former tramroad, near Tonna, West Glamorgan. Cambridge University Collection, CBZ 40: March 1977.

taining it in good condition is to make oneself responsible for a potential hazard. It is possible that the farmer whose sheep can be seen peacefully grazing in the fields close to the viaduct has acquired the viaduct for virtually nothing, as a means of gaining possession of the land underneath. British Rail would certainly have welcomed the opportunity of getting rid of it at almost any price. But it is equally possible that the farmer would prefer the risk of falling masonry to be carried by somebody else, secure in the knowledge that he would be bound to receive compensation if one of his animals or employees were to be killed or injured by part of the viaduct which had become loose. Closing a railway is by no means a simple matter. This photograph draws attention to both the opportunities and the drawbacks.

Route of a former tramroad, near Tonna, West Glamorgan

Tramroads, that is, waggon railways, are known to have existed in the North-East of England and the Midlands at the beginning of the seventeenth century, for taking coal from the pits to loading-points on navigable rivers. For motive power, the tramroads relied on both horses and gravity. In the seventeenth, and most of the eighteenth century, the waggons ran on wooden rails, fixed to stone blocks, with the top surface of the rails reinforced by strips of cast iron. Towards the end of the eighteenth century, there was a gradual change-over from wooden to cast-iron rails. These were of two types – edge-rails, for waggons fitted with the kind of flanged wheels which are universal today, and plate-rails, of L-shaped section, for vehicles with flangeless wheels.

Edge-rails first came into use *c*. 1790. They were made in 36-inch lengths, fish-bellied to give them extra strength. They often broke, a problem not solved until wrought-iron rails were successfully introduced *c* 1825. Plate-rails had many disadvantages, including increased friction and therefore wear, and an accumulation of dust and stones in the angle, but their shape endowed them with inherent strength and they could be given continuous support on baulks of timber. They were first used *c*. 1788 and, for a while, spread all over Britain, except in the North-East.

They were particularly popular in South Wales.

The tramroad shown in **85** is near Tonna, Glamorgan. It was about 1.5 km long, and ran to Castell-fford-nant, on the Neath Canal. The Neath Valley was served by the Neath and Tennant Canals, the junction of which was at Aberdulais. Neath had been an important centre of the copper-smelting industry since the 1580s and subsequently smelted silver and lead ores from Cardiganshire. The two canals made it possible for both the ores and the fuel with which to smelt them to be brought easily and cheaply to Neath. A number of tramroads were constructed to link the canals with nearby pits, often at the expense of the canal company and as a condition of obtaining permission to build the canal. The history of this particular tramroad is obscure, but it may well have been constructed and maintained under some such arrangement. Its date, also, cannot be established with any certainty, but it is likely to have been within the second decade of the nineteenth century.

One can see from the photograph that considerable grading work was necessary, by means of a cutting and an embankment. The pit waste-tips have been mostly levelled, but they must have been close to the buildings at the top of the picture. The evidence of tramroads branching off the main line, at the bottom of the photograph, suggests that there may have been a second group of pits within this area.

Airports and airfields

During the early days of aviation – which means, for practical purposes, up to 1930 – both civil and military aircraft operated from grass airfields, without hard runways. The aeroplanes were very small by today's standards and, even when they were fully loaded, they were light enough to take off from a reasonably level and well-drained field, provided the grass was not too long. When they were in difficulties, they often made an emergency landing on a farmer's field without harming the passengers or damaging the aeroplane very much.

Most of these early airfields – airports is much too grand a term for them – have now been built over, or converted into sports grounds. Even if hard landing and take-off strips had been provided, they would have been far too small to accommodate the kind of aircraft in use today and, closely ringed with housing estates as they usually became during the 1920s and 1930s, they would have been an intolerable nuisance, given the noise level of modern planes landing and taking off at the frequent intervals which are normal nowadays. Before 1939, flights were few, take-off and landing distances were short, and an aeroplane was considered 'giant' if it carried more than fifty people.

Shoreham Airport, in Sussex, is the best place at which to get a good impression of flying in its developing days. With a history going back to 1916, and still in use, it has a longer history of running scheduled passenger flights than any other airport in the world. There was, until 1982, no hard runway – local residents had opposed it – and the terminal buildings are more reminiscent of the clubhouse at a golf course than of anything we should think of as an airport today.

But at Shoreham we can learn almost nothing from a conventional aerial photograph that we could not discover equally well on the ground and much the same is true of any former all-grass airfield. For those with hard runways, however, the situation is different. Britain is covered with the vestiges of wartime airfields. Many of the smaller ones, constructed to serve fighter aircraft, were comparatively simple affairs, with a single tarmac or concrete runway and, branching off it, a num-

ber of approach runways leading to the hangars and ground circles where the aircraft were parked. Once abandoned, as they were very soon after 1945, most of these airfields were returned to some form of agriculture, although the pattern of hard strips has made cultivation difficult. Removing what are in effect roads and restoring the fields completely to their original use is an expense which the Government has, with rare exceptions, refused to handle and which the land-owners cannot afford. But, after forty years, the tarmac has cracked and mellowed, grass and weeds have grown through and the normal process of nature taking over has operated to a certain extent. Aerial photographs, however, leave one in no doubt about the years of wartime occupation, with the remains of protective embankments, air-raid shelters and old Nissen huts, often used for farm purposes, to add to the evidence.

It is, however, in suburban areas that aerial photography really comes into its own, as a means of revealing the traces of old hard-runway airfields which have been built over. Two classic instances of this are at Croydon and at Whitchurch, on the outskirts of Bristol.

Britain's oldest operational airport: Shoreham-by-Sea, West Sussex

Shoreham Airport is bounded by the A 27 to the north, the river Adur to the east, the railway to the south, and the built-up area of Lancing to the west. It cannot be expanded, and these permanent restrictions preclude the use of large aircraft. There are, even so, scheduled services to the Channel Islands and France and within the United Kingdom, with 12–30 seater aircraft, together with a good deal of business, charter and private flying.

The history of Shoreham Airport goes back to the beginning of flying in Britain. It was officially opened on 26 June 1911, and on 4 July of the same year the world's first cargo flight operated from here, when a box of electric light bulbs was carried from Shoreham to Hove. During the First

86 **Shoreham Airport, West Sussex.** Shoreham Airport archives, ref. 18-82-140: July 1982. Scale 1:7,600.

World War, the airfield was requisitioned for use by the Royal Flying Corps and, later, by the Royal Canadian Air Force. After the war, the Southern Aero Club, the oldest in the country, resumed its activities at Shoreham, and in 1930 the municipal authorities of Brighton, Hove and Worthing formed a joint committee to establish a municipal airport for the three towns. The new terminal building, which still functions, was opened in 1936, and until the outbreak of war in 1939 there were regular services to Bournemouth, Bristol, Cardiff, Croydon, Deauville, Jersey, Le Touquet, Liverpool, Ryde, Manchester and Portsmouth.

In 1939 the airport was taken over by the Air Ministry and, with Croydon now closed for civilian flying, Shoreham became the terminal for flights to Britain by the neutral countries of Belgium, France, Denmark and Holland, until they were invaded and occupied by the Germans. During the same period, the British wartime organisation, National Air Communications, operated services from Shoreham to Jersey, Guernsey, Dieppe, Paris, Tunis and Alexandria. For the remainder of the War, the airport was used by Fighter Command and for Air Sea Rescue duties.

After the War, during which the airport suffered a good deal of damage from air-raids, it was restored to civil use and operated, not very satisfactorily, by the Ministry of Defence until 1951. Passenger services were not successful and the Ministry tried to offset its expenses by leasing the

105

87 Shoreham Airport. Shoreham Airport archives 18-83-037: May 1983. Scale 1:7,600.

facilities to companies manufacturing light air-craft, to E. G. Miles Ltd from 1952 to 1960, and to Beagle Aircraft from 1960 to 1969. In 1971 Shoreham reverted to its pre-war status as a municipal airport and since then much has been done to make it an efficient and attractive civilian aviation centre.

Until very recently, Shoreham Airport suffered from the great disadvantage of having no hard runway. The airfield is only 1.8 m above sea-level and in wet weather, especially during the winter, it could not drain fast enough to allow flights to take off and land with the regularity which was necessary to provide the airport with a steady income. For many years local residents opposed the construction of a hard runway, in the mis-taken belief that it would result in the arrival of larger and noisier aircraft. This resistance was eventually overcome and in July 1982 Shoreham had its long-awaited runway, which has led to a great improvement in overall efficiency.

The new runway can be seen on **86**. This is one of a series of infra-red aerial photographs, com-missioned as part of a general survey of airfields in the southern counties, to see if any wartime mines were still buried there. The mines had been laid in order to damage the airfields in case of a German invasion and in some cases the number of mines removed after the War did not appear to coincide with the number laid. Any survivals could well have been revealed by infra-red photography.

106

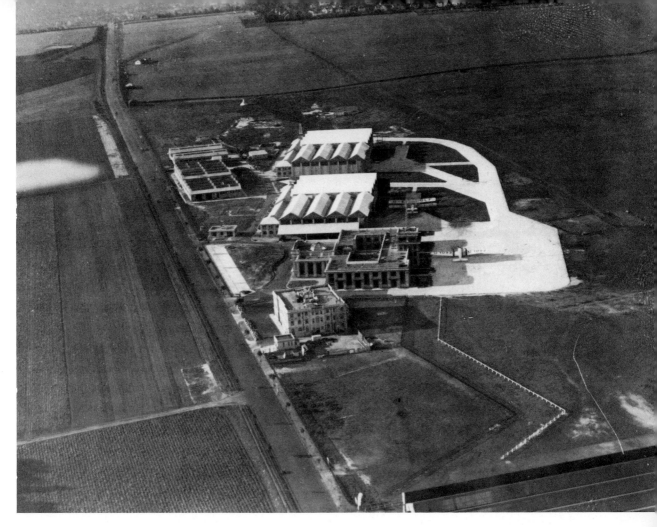

88 Croydon Airport, Surrey. Croydon Public Library: early 1930s.

The photographs taken at Shoreham failed to indicate the presence of any mines, but they made it possible to observe certain features which were not apparent in ordinary photographs. Chief among these was the main drain, which follows a roughly L-shaped course across the centre of the picture and leads the water away to the River Adur, the course of which can be seen running down the right-hand edge of the photograph. The new tarmac runway, 760 m long and 18 m wide, has been completed and follows almost the whole length of the western side of the airfield. The taxiing runway, linking the main runway to the terminal building, on the airfield's southern boundary, is also clearly visible. The light-coloured areas along both sides of the new runway represent soil excavated during the construction of the runway and not yet grassed over.

The large number of small aircraft parked in front of the terminal buildings provide evidence of Shoreham's popularity as a centre of private flying. Under dry conditions, aircraft of this size would normally use one of Shoreham's three grass runways, one of which is very obvious on **86**. A later infra-red picture, **87**, shows the pattern of grass runways much more completely, mainly because the soil temperature was higher and the runways more closely mown than when the previous photograph was taken. Similar reasons account for the curiously different appearance of the large area near the river, in the north-eastern corner of the airfield.

Croydon Airport, Surrey

Croydon was a military aerodrome during the First World War. In 1918 the National Aircraft Factory was built on a site close to the airfield, in what is now Purley Way. Croydon was formally adopted as the Customs airport for London in succession to Hounslow in 1920. It made do with temporary facilities until 1928, when its new and, for the time, very grand permanent terminal

107

89 **Croydon Airport.** Croydon Public Library: early 1930s.

building was opened. During the Second World War, Croydon was closed to civilian traffic and became an important centre of RAF operations. It suffered severely from wartime bombing and most of the hangars were destroyed or badly damaged.

It finally ceased functioning as an airport in 1959. The terminal building was put up for sale and is at present being used as a cash-and-carry furniture warehouse. The airfield has been largely built over. The Aerodrome Hotel remains, and has, indeed, been considerably extended.

Photographs **88** and **89** were taken at some time in the early 1930s. They appear to have been taken by a passenger from an aircraft about to land. There must be thousands of such photographs in existence, and, if one were able to locate them, they would form an invaluable addition to the archives of aerial photography. Photograph **88** gives a good impression of the layout of the airport. Purley Way, the road serving the airport, runs through what, at this point, is still to a great extent an agricultural landscape, although, as one can see, suburbia is encroaching fast. The road, incidentally, has remarkably little traffic on it.

The Aerodrome Hotel is the square, flat-roofed building nearest to the bottom of the picture and to the terminal building. The hangars are the two blocks of buildings beyond it, linked to the airport apron by hard runways. There were never any hard runways on the airfield itself. From the beginning to the end of Croydon's career, the aircraft took off and landed on grass. Even with hard runways, the airfield would not have been big enough to take the bigger and heavier planes which were coming into service in the 1950s and in its last days it was used virtually as a flying club.

Photograph **89** shows the front of the terminal building, one of the largest in the world at the time when it was opened. The public viewing enclosure is behind the Aerodrome Hotel and to the right of it. With its white-painted fence, it reminds one of a racecourse and, during the 1920s

90 Croydon Airport: industrial development. Cambridge University Collection, CPY 48: August 1983.

and 1930s, aerodromes did indeed have a markedly sporting flavour about them. A further group of hangars is visible on the right-hand edge of the photograph.

Both photographs make two additional points very well. The first is that the airport handled very few flights each day. The two aircraft which one can see in **88** are quite typical of what Croydon expected to have to handle at any one time. In 1932, which is approximately when these photographs were taken, 70,000 passengers passed through Croydon, or roughly 200 a day. This hardly suggests either that the staff were seriously over-worked or that local residents had much to complain about in the matter of noise. By 1937, the number of passengers had risen to something like 400 a day and even that does not seem likely to have strained resources unduly.

When flying came to an end at Croydon, the property was divided among a number of different users. About a quarter was allocated to private and municipal housing and to schools, and one-eighth to factories and warehouses, and the remainder was left for playing fields and a public open space. The industrial development, which took place in the area immediately adjoining the old terminal building, is shown on **90**. The terminal remains and so does the Aerodrome Hotel, with an extra wing added, on its left. All the other buildings are new.

Apart from the terminal, the only surviving evidence of what was once the centre of British civil aviation are two small fragments of taxiing runway in the top right-hand corner of the picture.

109

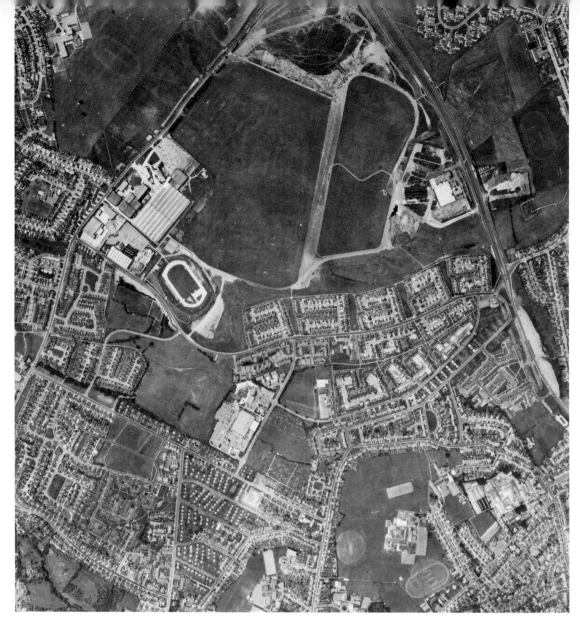

91 Whitchurch Airport, Avon: industrial and recreational development. Cambridge University Collection, RC8-EO 224: July 1982. Scale 1:11,750.

Whitchurch Airport, Avon

Bristol's airport at Whitchurch was opened in 1930 and it continued in service until 1957, when the present airport at Lulsgate replaced it. It was owned by the Corporation of Bristol, which bought 120 ha for the purpose, and administered by the City Council. In 1939 it was requisitioned by the Department of Civil Aviation and the whole of the Imperial Airways fleet was moved there from Croydon for the duration of the War. Most of the Government's transatlantic flights between 1939 and 1945 used Whitchurch as a base.

After the War it was decided that the airport was unsuitable for development, to accommodate the larger aeroplanes coming into use, and it was eventually closed and the terminal building demolished. The hard runways which had been constructed to meet wartime requirements can, however, still be seen.

Most of the former airfield is now a recreation ground, known as Hengrove Park, but three areas around the perimeter were scheduled for development, one for housing, one for industry and one for Whitchurch Sports Centre. This development is well shown in **91**. The airfield area occupies most of the left-hand side of the photograph.

92 Gatwick Airport, West Sussex: the circular terminal building (Beehive). Gatwick Airport photograph, taken by Alan Timbrell: 1936.

Whitchurch Sports Centre is at its bottom right, and the five blocks of housing to the north of it have absorbed a large slice of the right-hand edge of the former airfield. The new ring road, nostalgically named Airport Way, cuts through the upper part of the airfield, with some industrial development on both sides of it.

Bristol has not been fortunate, or perhaps wise, in the choice of sites for its airport. Whitchurch, although conveniently close to the centre of Bristol, was always too much surrounded by housing estates for safety and comfort. Its successor, at Lulsgate, suffers greatly from problems of fog and low cloud, and the cost of extending its runways, in order to allow it to take the new types of aircraft which were coming into service during the 1960s and 1970s, was very high.

When he opened Whitchurch Airport on 31 May 1930, Prince George, as he then was, said, 'It needs little imagination to foresee the future of this airport. In time, it is certain to become an important junction for air routes between London and Ireland and many large towns in the West of England and Wales.' His Royal Highness, unfor-

tunately for Bristol, was over-optimistic. From an aviation point of view, the city's pre-war promise has never been realised. There are very few more scheduled flights from Lulsgate than there were from Whitchurch and, over the year, holiday charter flights make up the bulk of the traffic. Had aircraft remained small, the answer might well have been different. Whitchurch could still be in use and 20-seater planes could be transporting passengers around the British Isles in the way Prince George prophesied.

Photograph **91** shows a dream that went wrong.

Gatwick Airport, West Sussex

London's principal pre-war passenger airport, at Croydon, was surrounded by houses and too small for the aircraft which were beginning to come into service in the 1950s. With its undulating grass landing field, it was inadequate as a major airport even in the 1930s and by 1939 it had been outclassed by several European airports. Gatwick,

93 Gatwick Airport: **closer view of the Beehive.** British Airports Authority photograph, taken by Alan Timbrell: 1983.

officially opened in 1936, was on a more suitable site and had space to grow. It also had the great advantage of being close to a main railway line into London.

There has been an airfield at Gatwick since 1930, when an aerodrome for private flying was opened about a mile south of the present terminal building. In 1934 it was licensed as a public airport, under the name of London South (Gatwick). Gatwick from the beginning was an altogether more modern and adventurous airport than Croydon. The original circular terminal building is shown in **92**, taken in 1936, the year in which it was opened. This pioneering terminal was popularly known as the Beehive. Six corridors with telescopic canopies radiated from a central passenger concourse, so that six aircraft could be dealt with at the same time. Designed by Hoar, Marlow and Lovett, it is still in existence, although nowadays it is used only for office and training purposes. Photograph **93**, a recent low-

level aerial photograph, shows the Beehive in greater detail, with its former control room as the cherry on top of the bun.

Gatwick, like Croydon, had no hard runway in the 1930s. As one can see from the 1936 photograph, only the area immediately surrounding the terminal building and the hangars had a concrete surface. The railway station serving the airport is at centre right. It was linked to the passenger terminal by means of a tunnel. Gatwick was the first airport in the world to have its own railway station.

During the Second World War, Gatwick was used by the RAF as a fighter station. After the war it was chosen by the Government as the site for London's second major airport, mainly to serve as a base for the independent airlines, but also to take diversions from Heathrow. Development for this began in 1956 and the original airport, with the Beehive, ceased to operate in that year.

94 Gatwick: the new airport. British Airports Authority photograph, taken by Alan Timbrell: 1958.

The new airport was officially opened in June 1958. It was built partly on the former Gatwick racecourse, with the terminal building, designed by Yothe, Rosenberg and Mardall, on the site of the grandstand. The racecourse had its own railway station, which was used as the basis of the new Gatwick Airport station. The platform originally serving the airport miraculously still survives.

Gatwick's new airport was the first in Europe to have a pier along which passengers walked to their aircraft, although America had had this facility for some time. Extensions both to the terminal and the runways were carried out during the 1960s and 1970s, and a circular satellite was opened in April 1983. It is connected to the main terminal by a rapid transit system, a monorail, which is the first of its kind at any airport outside the United States. A second terminal, to be known as the North Terminal, to the north-west of Terminal 1, is now under construction. The two terminals will also have a monorail link.

The changes which have taken place at Gatwick since 1956 are illustrated by **94**, **95**, **96** and **97**. Photograph **94**, taken in 1958, shows the new airport in the year it opened. The 1936 airport is at left centre, with its railway station already gone. By 1978, as shown in **95**, considerable development has taken place, especially on the eastern side of the railway, opposite the terminal. The multi-storey car-park, joined to the terminal by two passenger bridges, is an integrated part of the complex and an intricate road pattern allows quick and easy access to the main highway system.

Photograph **96**, taken in 1983, shows the satellite in operation. The Gatwick Hilton has been built in front of the car park. Another storey has been added to the main terminal building, a feature which is seen more easily in **97**, also taken in 1983. This photograph gives a good impression of the piers, and of the monorail link between the satellite and the terminal (see also Fig. 5).

95 Gatwick Airport: twenty years later than 94. British Airports Authority, LGW 6274, taken by Alan Timbrell: June 1978.

96 Gatwick Airport: the circular satellite. British Airports Authority photograph, taken by Alan Timbrell: 1983.

97 Gatwick Airport: close-up view of the circular satellite. British Airports Authority, LGW 8434, taken by Alan Timbrell: 1983.

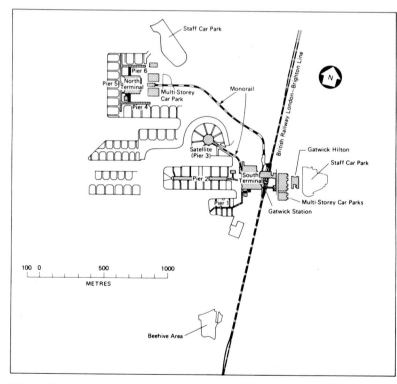

Fig. 5 Gatwick Airport: position of terminals and satellite.

New towns and model villages

'New Towns' is not a precise term, although any alternative to it is likely to be both lengthy and clumsy. During the past century it has been used to describe three different types of urban development – a town set up and financed as a private enterprise; a public venture established under Government control and with Government money on a site where there was previously no settlement at all, and a Government-supported town constructed around the nucleus of a previously existing, but small community. The second and third types are post-Second World War concepts, while the first dates back to the nineteenth century.

All three varieties of New Town have been based on the policy of allowing people to live close to their work. The earliest examples were constructed by benevolent employers, usually in the textile industry, for whom it was natural to plan living accommodation within easy travelling distance of the mill or factory. In such cases, the families in these model settlements were dependent on a single employer for a livelihood. New Towns in the modern sense have been created on different assumptions. In every instance, one or more areas of the site have been reserved for what is loosely called industrial development. 'Industrial' does not necessarily mean 'factories', however. It may, and often does, include warehousing, research institutes, and vehicle repair centres. All manufacturing is of the kind referred to as 'light'; that is, it does not produce noise or atmospheric pollution. The New Towns of the past forty years do not accommodate, for example, chemical factories or steelworks. They aim at providing as wide a range of employment as possible, partly as a safeguard against economic vicissitudes and partly in order to encourage a reasonable balance of occupations and social classes within the town.

With the same hope of achieving a social variety, the New Town planners have taken care to offer a range of housing possibilities. Broadly speaking, houses for sale have been intended for management and for those in other middle-class occupations, and houses to let for what is often termed the shop-floor, but the difference is, inevitably, not clear-cut, and in any case the balanced-population policy is frustrated by the wish of many people to work in the New Town but to live outside it, often at a considerable distance. The reverse is also true. In all the New Towns so far built, a considerable proportion of the people who live in them work elsewhere. To that extent, these towns have become what they were theoretically not intended to be, commuting centres.

In the case of towns, such as Peterborough, which have been developed rapidly, rather than created from nothing, a third type of inhabitant can be distinguished, the Old Residents. These are the original population, the families who were there before the New Town arrived to absorb them and who have often, in many cases, bitterly resented the changed style of life which has been thrust upon them.

Aerial photography can hardly help to document commuting or resentment, but it is of great value in showing how and how fast the town has spread and in illustrating how the planners' minds worked. It is an excellent tool for revealing the bones of the New Town.

Creswell, a late Victorian mining village in Derbyshire

Creswell, 16 km east-north-east of Chesterfield, was a small, scattered village until the middle of the nineteenth century. The area was almost entirely agricultural and the principal landowner was the Duke of Portland. Coal-mining began here in the 1860s, greatly helped by the good railway connections – Creswell was served by both the London, Midland and Scottish and the London and North-Eastern Railways.

The model village for miners and their families was built between 1896 and 1900 on the initiative of Percy Halton, of the Bolsover Mining Company. Photograph **98** shows the highly original layout of the original scheme, with the houses built on both sides of a road running around a hexagon. The centre of the area enclosed by the hexagon was left as an open space, with the inner ring of houses facing on to it, and the outer ring

117

98 Creswell, Derbyshire. Cambridge University Collection, CCG 51: May 1977.

looking outwards. A service road between the backs of the two rings provides easy service access.

Allotments, to be seen in the bottom half of the picture, took the place of the vegetable gardens which the miners expected and would normally have had at the back of their houses. There were formerly many more of these, but a number have gone in order to provide what is now the town of Creswell with a sports ground, at right centre of the photograph. Others have had to yield place to a car park, visible just below the sports field. The nineteenth-century planners were not required to think of car-parking. In 1896 miners travelled by train or on foot.

The houses in the top half of the picture are more modern and have, it will be noticed, gardens attached to them in the traditional way.

A twentieth-century village: Bar Hill, Cambridgeshire

In 1967, Bar Hill village, 6.5 km out of Cambridge on the Huntingdon side, was described as 'probably the most ambitious private housing development in the country'.[1] The project was undertaken by Cubitts, and the original scheme involved the construction of 1,250 houses, a supermarket and 40 shops, an office block, church and two schools, as well as an industrial estate. It was reckoned that the whole project would take eight years to complete and that eventually 4,000 people would live there, a figure which would appear to put Bar Hill in the category of a small town, rather than a village.

Apart from having been planned as a unit, Bar Hill has a number of unusual features. The single

99 Bar Hill, Cambridgeshire. Cambridge University Collection, RC8–T 106: 1970. Scale 1:13,100.

church is interdenominational, with services, educational work and study groups run jointly by the Church of England and the Free Churches; and community activities of all kinds are organised by a Village Trust, the members of which are all elected. The houses, which are of several different sizes and types, are named after Cambridge colleges. A Clare, for instance, is a three-bedroomed terraced house, and a Trinity a four-bedroomed town house.

In 1971 the total population of Bar Hill was 674, living in 200 separate households, and by 1981 the number of inhabitants was 2,445. The creation of the village has, in other words, not proceeded as fast and as far as was originally intended, although progress has been steady. At

100 Bar Hill. Cambridge University Collection, RC8–BQ 116: 1976. Scale 1:10,750.

present the number of people living in Bar Hill is rising at the rate of about 100 a year.

The four photographs **99, 100, 101** and **102**, show Bar Hill as it was in 1970, 1976, 1980 and 1982 respectively. The pattern of growth can be clearly seen. The village lies close to the A 604, and on the left-hand side of it as one travels from Cambridge to Huntingdon. If one considers the

site to be divided into four quarters, the north-western, south-western and south-eastern quarters are reserved for housing and the north-eastern for shops and industry. A feature of the north-eastern quarter which was not included in the original plan is the 100-room Cambridgeshire Hotel, which can certainly be considered an industrial development and one which no doubt provides

101 Bar Hill. Cambridge University Collection, RC8–DO 64: 1980. Scale 1:16,800.

employment opportunities for people living in the village.

It remains true, however, that most families in Bar Hill do not derive their income from the village. What Cubitts have provided is not a self-contained community, but an exceptionally well-planned commuting centre conveniently close to Cambridge. It would be surprising if, by 1995, all the land reserved for housing at Bar Hill had not been taken up. This is what an aerial photograph taken in that year would almost certainly show. It is doubtful, however, if there will have been any considerable expansion within the shopping–industrial area.

Reference

1. Robert Troop, in *The Sunday Times*, 28 May 1967.

121

102 **Bar Hill.** Cambridge University Collection, RC8-EI 30: 1982. Scale 1:14,700.

Cumbernauld New Town, Strathclyde

Cumbernauld was designated a New Town in 1956. Up to that time it had been a small community of 3,600 people. By 1982 it had 48,000 inhabitants, which is two-thirds of the total originally aimed at. The planning differs from that of earlier New Towns in two respects. The use of three categories of road helps to keep the traffic free-flowing, without the use of traffic lights or police. An urban motorway runs through the centre of the town and the rest of the network consists of what are known as distributor roads and local feeder roads. A network of walkways allows pedestrians to cross roads by means of bridges and underpasses. Cumbernauld's second distinguishing feature is the concentration of all main commercial and social activities into a single

103 Cumbernauld New Town, Strathclyde: the non-industrial area. Cambridge University Collection, BGB 45: July 1971.

complex of buildings, a so-called 'megastructure' in the city centre.

Two-thirds of the population originally lived in Glasgow and many still work there. Cumbernauld itself provides employment for about 13,000 people, of whom 4,000 live elsewhere. Slightly more than 11,000 travel to work in Glasgow, which is a ¾-hour journey by car.

Photograph 103 gives a general impression of the non-industrial area of the town. The policy has been to keep all industrial development on the periphery. The varied character of the housing is evident, ranging as it does from terraced houses to flats in tower blocks. About forty per cent of all accommodation is owner-occupied, a figure considerably less than the average for the United Kingdom, though rather higher than for Scotland as a whole. The routes of the urban motorway, to the left of the tower blocks, and of the distributor roads can be easily followed.

Photograph 104 shows the Cumbernauld Centre and its immediate surroundings in more detail. The walkways and their tunnels provide safe links between the residential areas and the centre, and

access to the numerous car parks also appears to be a simple matter. Every house in Cumbernauld, incidentally, has either a garage or an off-street parking place, although this may not be readily apparent from this photograph. It is, however, more easily appreciated from 105. This also shows part of the Lenziemill Industrial Area, which is in the course of development. Both pedestrian and vehicle access to this area are by bridges, which are the most effective way of crossing the railway line to Glasgow, which runs diagonally across the centre of the picture.

A passenger train standing at Cumbernauld station can be noticed here, and it is perhaps worth mentioning that, whatever else may be central and convenient for local residents, the railway station certainly is not. Its position represents a long walk for most people, a feature of the town which suggests that Cumbernauld has been planned mainly with a car-owning population in mind. The town's industries make virtually no use of the railway. Their transport is entirely road-based.

104 Cumbernauld New Town: the Cumbernauld Centre. Cumbernauld Development Corporation archive: March 1983.

Letchworth Garden City, Hertfordshire

During the nineteenth century, a number of paternalistic industrialists in Europe and America tried to provide their workers with agreeably spacious estates to live in, as an alternative to the degraded and filthy environment which had become associated with manufacturing industry. In Britain, Ebenezer Howard took this idea a stage further forward, by pointing out in his influential book, *Tomorrow*, published in 1898, that there was no solution within the boundaries of existing cities. One had to make completely new starts, by creating what came to be known as 'garden cities' in the countryside. These would have a socially balanced population and an environment in which pleasant working places and pleasant living conditions would be planned together.

When the opportunity arose to put his ideas into practice, they were nearly always misunderstood or debased. Only Letchworth and Welwyn, the first begun in 1904, with a density of only 12 houses to the acre, and the second in

1920, really achieved anything resembling the garden city, as Howard conceived it. The garden city, an integrated, functioning unit, was held to be impracticable and too expensive and the dormitory suburb and the council estate – the Garden Suburb was an earlier and superior version: Hampstead Garden Suburb was laid out from 1907 onwards – replaced it, as truncated, anaemic versions of the original.

The plan prepared by the architects for the First Garden City Company in 1904 is shown in Fig. 6. The railway linking London with Cambridge and Peterborough runs through the centre of the site. The same railway served Welwyn Garden City, closer to London. The architects of Letchworth and Welwyn saw good railway communication as an essential element in their overall plan. With this in mind, the railway station was within easy walking distance of anywhere within the residential part of the town and the factory area was well served by railway sidings.

Ebenezer Howard assumed a town which would be compact, so that the people living in it could

124

105 Cumbernauld New Town: the Lenziemill Industrial Area. Cumbernauld Development Corporation: March 1983.

walk to school, to work and to the shops without any undue expenditure of time or energy. It was a pre-car concept and the aerial photograph, **106** shows what has happened since.

The basic plan has stood the test of time remarkably well. Housing density is still low, every house has a respectable garden and most journeys within the town could still be accomplished on foot by a reasonably able-bodied person without difficulty, given the willingness to do so. But there are one or two significant pointers to change. The industrial area has extended to the other side of the railway track and there are signs that within ten years or so in-filling will have produced a continuously built-up area towards the settlements in the top right-hand corner of the photograph. More important, the Garden City is beginning to lose its organic quality. It is in the process of creating its own suburbs, without social amenities of their own, yet just too far from the central area to be able to identify with it.

And, within the main industrial sector of the town, there is now not a trace of a railway siding.

A New Town in the West Midlands: Telford, Shropshire

Telford, established with its Development Corporation in 1968, is an amalgam of a completely new community and the existing towns of Wellington, Oakengates, Dawley, Madeley and Ironbridge, together with a number of villages and hamlets. It is 30 km from Wolverhampton, 56 km from Birmingham and 24 km from Shrewsbury. The M 54, which runs more or less through the middle of it, provides a direct link to the M 6. Since Telford was founded, the population has increased by more than 37,000 to over 107,000 and is expected to rise to about 130,000 by the end of the 1990s. Over the fifteen years, 18,000 houses have been built to accommodate the town's new residents.

Photograph **107** shows part of the area as it was in June 1979. The River Severn runs through the Ironbridge Gorge up the right-hand edge of the picture, with the Iron Bridge itself visible as a white line across the river. Going north from the

125

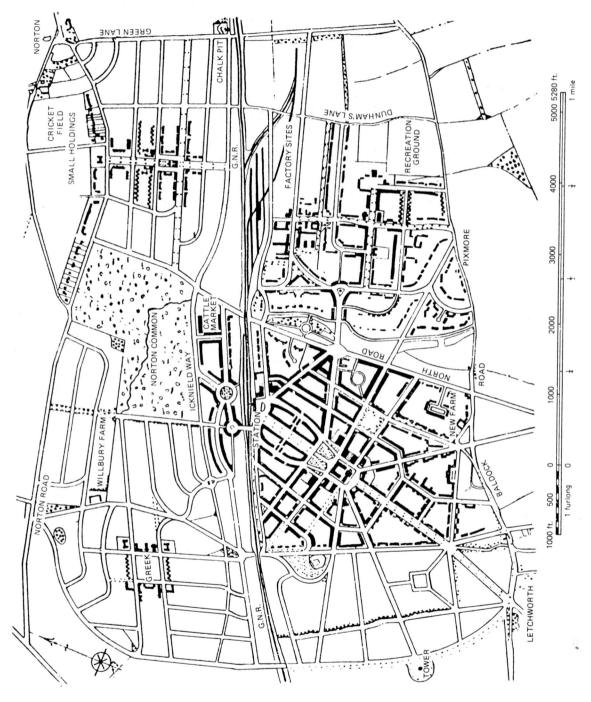

Fig. 6 Letchworth Garden City: the 1904 plan.

106 Letchworth Garden City, Hertfordshire. Letchworth Museum and Art Gallery collection: 1976.

river, up the left-hand side of this aerial photo-graph is the A 4169, which has the Coalbrookdale Furnace and Museum of Iron on its left, just before it swings right across the centre of the picture. To the left of the A 4169 and on the other side of the Coalbrookdale works, one can see the railway from Buildwas Junction to Shifnal, which crosses the picture very prominently from left to right.

The New Town area with its agreeable patterns of houses south of the railway is Woodside. To the right of it and extending up to the right-hand edge of the photograph is part of the older town of Madeley and below it, in the bottom right-hand corner, is Blists Hill, with the entrance to the Open Air Museum and the buildings sheltering the old beam engines close by.

Apart from Woodside's housing patterns – those of Madeley are far less organised and con-trolled, as befits an old town – three features of this part of Telford are particularly worth attention. The first is the astonishing amount of woodland, which needs an aerial photograph to do it justice. This, and the hilly nature of the terrain, provides Telford with a much more interesting and attrac-tive site than most of the other New Towns have at their disposal. The second piece of illumi-nation which comes from studying a photograph of this kind is the astonishing numbers of quarries and waste dumps which one sees dotted about the picture, a useful reminder that this is an old indus-trial area. The third feature of special interest concerns the numbers of schools and playing fields, often in association. Since this is a summer-time picture, there are a number of cricket squares in evidence. The most remarkable con-centration of leisure facilities is to be found on the right centre edge of the picture, below the large belt of trees. This forms the Madison Edu-cation and Recreation Centre. Here, close together, there are a sports ground, bowling club, tennis courts and an artificial ski-slope. The residents of Telford are well provided for in this respect.

127

107 **Telford, Shropshire.** Photographed for Telford Development Corporation by Cartographical Services (Southampton) Ltd.; sortie no. 830, print no. 5105: June 1979. Scale 1:20,900.

New Rossington, a mining town in South Yorkshire

New Rossington, 8 km south-east of Doncaster, is a largely twentieth-century creation, designed to house mining families who worked in the pit, which was sunk in 1912 and produced its first coal in 1915. It was an exceptionally imaginative pro-

ject, providing excellent living conditions for the community which obtained its livelihood from the colliery. The population is now more than 13,000, a figure which entitles New Rossington to be considered a town, rather than the village it is frequently called.

The village of Rossington, or Old Rossington, has existed since early medieval times – the

108 New Rossington, South Yorkshire. Cambridge University Collection, CCL 31: June 1977. Scale 1:16,600.

church contains some twelfth-century work – but it has been overshadowed by New Rossington for many years.

The photograph **108**, shows the interesting layout of the town, which can be properly appreciated only from the air, and the generous proportion of the total area which has been allocated to parks and playing fields. Even more important is the evident care which has been taken to screen the mine workings, which are very close to the town. The thick belt of trees planted between the colliery and the residential areas makes it much easier for miners to forget their work once they are away from it. The overall concept represents industrial responsibility of a very high order and one should perhaps emphasise that the whole scheme was devised and put into action at a time when Britain's coal mines were privately owned, long before the days of the National Coal Board.

An expanded town: Peterborough, Cambridgeshire

Between 1145, when work began on the Cathedral, until 1845, when the railway arrived, Peterborough was a small market town, centred around a massive church. The railway changed the character of the town, by making it possible for engineering firms to base themselves in Peterborough, which became one of the most important rail junctions in Britain, with good connections to London, the Midlands and the North-West, the North-East and Scotland. Railway workshops came first and they were followed in the present century, first by Baker Perkins, manufacturers of baking equipment, and then, in 1932, by Perkins Engines.

After the Second World War, the danger of relying on a small number of traditional industries was becoming apparent and the decision was taken to broaden the base of the town's activity

129

109 Peterborough, Cambridgeshire. Cambridge University Collection, RC8–CN 10: May 1978. Scale 1: 16,600.

and to considerably expand its population. Peterborough was officially designated a New Town in 1967 and a Development Corporation was established in 1968 to carry through such a programme. Its efforts have been very successful. A large number of manufacturing companies have been attracted to the area and commercial and professional firms such as Thomas Cook and the Pearl Assurance Company have transferred their headquarters here. During the same period, Peterborough has been transformed as a regional shopping centre.

Between 1967 and 1982, the population increased from a little over 81,000 to 124,000, the labour force from 45,000 to 68,000, and the number of houses from 32,750 to nearly 48,000.

130

110 Peterborough: the Queensgate shopping centre under construction. Peterborough Development Corporation archive, P3963/14: 1981.

Photograph **109** shows the way in which the Longthorpe area of the town had been developed from green fields by 1978. The district is bounded by Nene Parkway, the A 1260, to the west, Stoke Parkway, the A 47, to the north, and Longthorpe Parkway, the A 1179, to the south. Much care has been devoted to preserving open spaces. Thorpe Wood, bisected by the A 1260, lies just to the south-east of the roundabout at centre left, with

Thorpe Wood Golf Course just below it – the bunkers are clearly visible. There was a special reason for keeping what is now the golf course as an open space. It contains an important Roman site, which archaeologists may well wish to investigate again at some time in the future and, if development had been permitted here, that chance would have gone for ever. The fact that many tons of earth have been tipped on parts of

131

the site, in order to create bunkers, is of no great importance. The archaeology is perfectly safe underneath them.

Thorpe Hall, with Thorpe Park surrounding it, is at right centre, north of the A 1179. The River Nene cuts diagonally across the bottom right-hand corner of the photograph and since the picture was taken a dead-straight rowing and canoeing course has been dug out from the fields just south of the A 1179, fed from a channel leading from the River Nene.

Photograph **110** shows the Queensgate shopping centre under construction in 1981. It opened in the following year. The Cathedral remains intact near the top right-hand edge of the picture, but much of the centre of the old town, on the near side of the Cathedral, was cleared to make room for the new Centre. The great names – the John Lewis Partnership, Boots, Littlewoods – are now all installed there, as they are in most similar central redevelopment schemes, and there are, of course, large multi-storey car parks. Running across the centre of the picture, with Queensgate Centre just above it, is Bourges Boulevard, as a reminder of Peterborough's twin-town in France, and below it the railway station. Cowgate, leading up from the new roundabout towards the Guildhall and the Cathedral, is on the right-hand edge of the picture.

Those who knew the old city would find the new centre of Peterborough unrecognisable. This aerial picture may help them to discover their bearings.

The essence of aerial photography

The sites described and analysed in the preceding pages represent, of course, only a very small selection of the possibilities. They do, however, indicate a number of the ways in which aerial photography can be of use to the industrial historian, by allowing him to acquire a feeling for the site as a whole, by showing one feature in relation to another, by placing a town, a district or a factory within the context of available transport facilities, by providing a sense of overall scale, which is much more difficult to obtain at ground level, and, perhaps most important of all, by demonstrating growth and development.

Those who take photographs from the air possess one very great advantage over those who remain on the ground. They cannot trespass, be forbidden entry, or be ordered off the premises. Nobody owns the air-space above his house or his factory and the pilot or photographer, provided he has given the necessary notice to the air traffic authorities, and received their approval, may fly where he pleases. If he should happen to take photographs of Defence establishments, he cannot publish them without permission, but otherwise he is free to use his photographs in any way he chooses. This, at least, is the situation in the United Kingdom. Many other countries, especially in the Eastern Bloc, are not so indulgent.

Much of the value of aerial photography, as of photography in general, is accidental. A photograph may be taken for one purpose and used, possibly many years afterwards, for another. This inevitably makes indexing and cataloguing a difficult business, since one cannot possibly foresee what future researchers will find interesting. Picture librarians know this all too well. An old photograph listed, absolutely correctly, under 'Royal visit to Bethnal Green, 1925', may contain invaluable information about tramcars, costume, or street-trading. Similarly, an aerial photograph taken primarily to show the plan of an abandoned medieval village may also offer evidence of a disused railway.

It may be useful to remind ourselves of what a photograph, any photograph, is – a slice of time frozen by the camera. If we say that we have a photograph of, say, Liverpool docks, what we really mean is that we have a picture of the docks taken from an aeroplane at a particular time on a particular day in a particular year, from a particular height at a particular angle in a particular light. Another combination of these variables would have produced a different picture, as would the decision to use colour instead of black and white. One can only describe and interpret what one sees, and a photograph taken on Monday can easily provide different information and induce different attitudes and opinions from one taken on Tuesday.

The scientific ideal would certainly be photographs taken over a long period of time. That ideal is probably approached by American military analysts, studying satellite pictures of Russian missile sites, in a situation where money is of no importance. Lesser mortals unfortunately have to content themselves with more modest resources and to squeeze as much information as they can from the photographs which are available to them.

A number of the photographs reproduced in the present book are good examples of what one might call secondary usefulness. The indexing in Cambridge by the Committee for Aerial Photography is, in fact, exceptionally good, but several of the best photographs relating to industrial sites have been discovered by accident, simply by browsing through the files or by touching a chord in the excellent memory of the Curator. As a piece of academic research equipment, aerial photography has in the past primarily served the purposes of archaeologists whose interests lay within the traditional fields of the subject, not those of industrial archaeologists. One should emphasise, however, that the Committee is doing everything possible to remedy this situation. Many of the photographs used here were, in fact, taken specially for the present book, and contributing to the industrial record will undoubtedly form an important part of the work of the Committee in the years to come. Those responsible for its activities are determined that this shall be so. Industrial Britain is far too rich, profitable and interesting a seam to leave unexploited.

Bibliography

Industrial History from the Air is a pioneering book and the only kind of bibliography really appropriate to it is one which lists the sources of information which have been of assistance to the author in his choice and interpretation of the photographs. Aerial pictures are of value only when they are studied in conjunction with the documentary material relating to the sites and, in many cases, this is of a very fragmentary nature. It is unusual for the history of industrial concerns to be written in terms of their sites and their buildings and the literature relating to this aspect of a firm's development or decline was remarkably slender, until industrial archaeologists began to create it from the 1960s onwards. Once it became respectable, however, to work outwards from the physical evidence of industry and to use the information gained in this way as a supplement, and not infrequently as a corrective, to what the economic, social and technical historians had already discovered, a fuller and more satisfying understanding of the past became possible.

There is no essential difference between an aerial photograph of Swindon railway works and an aerial photograph of the site of a lost medieval village. In both cases, one is looking for information which is not apparent or recognisable for what it is to someone standing on the ground and, in order to obtain this, one has to learn how to extract full value from the new perspective which the low-flying aeroplane provides. The best book for acquiring the grammar of aerial photography is D. R. Wilson's *Air Photo Interpretation for Archaeologists* (1982). By showing what can be seen in photographs of a wide range of archaeological sites, one or two of them relating to industry and transport, Mr Wilson's very useful primer makes clear the possibilities of this way of looking at the activities and creations of the past.

So far as particular sites are concerned – the cement works at Westbury, and the Pedigree Petfoods factory at Melton Mowbray are typical examples – I have often had to rely mainly on information given to me by the firm in question, since very little published material exists. In other instances, I have been forced back onto books and articles I have written myself, a situation which is hardly ideal. For other sites and types of sites, however, authoritative works are available. Those which I have referred to a great deal are listed below. In most cases, the book includes a substantial bibliography. The industrial archaeology of areas represented by photographs used in this book is covered in detail and in a general way by D. Morgan Rees, *The Industrial Archaeology of Wales* (1975); John Butt, *The Industrial Archaeology of Scotland* (1967); Kenneth Hudson, *The Industrial Archaeology of Southern England* (2nd, revised edition, 1968); R. A. Buchanan and Neil Cossons, *The Industrial Archaeology of the Bristol Region* (1969); A. C. Todd and Peter Laws, *The Industrial Archaeology of Cornwall* (1972); Owen Ashmore, *The Industrial Archaeology of Lancashire* (1969).

For details of eighteenth- and nineteenth-century coal-mining, I have found much help in T. S. Ashton and J. Sykes, *The Coal Industry of the Eighteenth century* (1929); J. V. Nef, *Rise of the British Coal Industry*, 2 vols. (1932); F. Atkinson, *The Great Northern Coalfield 1700–1900* (1966); T. H. Hair's *Sketches of the Coal Mines in Northumberland and Durham* (1839, facsimile reprint 1969); and R. L. Galloway, *A History of Coal Mining in Great Britain* (1882, reprinted 1970). For the history of Chatterley Whitfield Colliery, the article by Peter Boreham in *Industrial Archaeology*, Vol. 14, No. 2, Summer 1979, is particularly valuable. A. R. Griffin's 'Industrial Archaeology as an aid to the study of mining history', in *Industrial Archaeology*, Vol. 11, No. 1, February 1974, has much of interest about bell-pits and other early techniques and emphasises the great difficulty of dating the surviving evidence of such mining.

Information about stone-quarrying in the relevant areas is to be found in M. B. Weinstock, *Old Dorset* (1967); Kenneth Hudson, *The Fashionable Stone: a History of the English Building Limestones* (1976); and Jean Lindsay, *A History of the North Wales Slate Industry* (1974). The development of the china-clay industry is described in R. M. Barton, *History of the China Clay Industry* (1966), and Kenneth Hudson, *The History of English China Clays* (1969).

For the history of river and canal navigation, I have found much help in T. S. Willan, *River Navigation in England, 1600–1750* (1936, reprinted 1964); Charles Hadfield, *British Canals: an Illustrated History* (1959, new edition 1966); K. R. Clew, *The Kennet and Avon Canal* (1968); and D. D. Gladwin, *The Canals of Britain* (1973).

The literature of railways is enormous and its quality very variable. I have relied especially on O. S. Nock, *The London and North Western Railway* (1960); H. Ellis, *The Midland Railway* (1953); H. Ellis, *British Railway History*, 2 vols. (1954, 1955); and J. Simmons, *The Railways of Britain* (1961). On the construction of railways, Terry Coleman, *The Railway Navvies* (1965) is unequalled. The development of the railway area in Swindon is described in Kenneth Hudson, 'The early years of the railway community in Swindon', *Transport History*, Vol. 1, No. 2, July 1968.

The growth of the Liverpool dock system is amply documented, except for the changes which have taken place during the past twenty years. I have made use of C. N. Parkinson, *The Rise of the Port of Liverpool* (1952); Quentin Hughes, *Seaport* (1964); W. Smith (ed.), *A Scientific Study of Merseyside* (1953); and G. Chandler, *An Illustrated History of Liverpool* (1972).

For facts about the Port of Bristol, I have gone to Bryan Little, *City and County of Bristol* (1954); W. G. Neale, *At the Port of Bristol*, Vol. 2: *The Turn of the Century, 1900–14* (1970). The archaeology of the Bristol City Docks has been carefully recorded, with good maps, by Robin Stiles, in 'Bristol city docks', *BIAS Journal*, Vol. 6, 1973.

The growth and decay of the Port of London can be

studied in R. Douglas Brown, *The Port of London* (1978); Sir Joseph G. Broadbank, *History of the Port of London*, 2 vols. (1921) and John Pudney, *London's Docks* (1975).

The development of the Port of Southampton is described by Dr L. E. Taverner in an article in *Economic Geography*, Vol. 26, No. 4, 1950, and further information can be found in the commemorative volume produced to coincide with the British Association meeting in Southampton in 1963: F. J. Monkhouse (ed.), *A Survey of Southampton and its Region* (1964). J. P. M. Pannell, who was Engineer to the Southampton Harbour Board, provides further details, especially of a technical nature, in his *Old Southampton Shores* (1967) and on pp. 161–70 of *An Illustrated History of Civil Engineering* (1964).

A number of specialist books have provided me with background material to the photographs which deal with industrial sites. The two works which have been of the greatest value in understanding the West of England cloth industry are J. de L. Mann, *The Cloth Industry of the West of England, 1640–1880* (1971), and K. G. Ponting, *History of the West of England Cloth Industry* (1957). Useful information concerning Lancashire's cotton mills and other buildings connected with the industry are to be found throughout Sir N. Pevsner, *The Buildings of England: Lancashire: The Industrial and Commercial South* (1964), although many of the buildings listed and described here have since been demolished. W. English, *The Textile Industry* (1969), is a good general account of the development of textile manufacturing in Britain, and so is J. N. Tann, *Working-Class Housing in Nineteenth-Century Britain* (1971).

Aerial photographs record industrial dereliction as no other medium can. *Derelict Land*, published by the Civic Trust in 1964, outlines and illustrates the problem and contains an excellent bibliography of books and articles on the subject. The same organisation's *Urban Wasteland* (1977) continued the campaign, this time in respect of land sterilised within cities and towns, rather than in the open countryside. The effects of industry on the landscape are given a broader historical perspective by R. Willward's *Lancashire: an Illustrated Essay on the History of the Landscape* (1955).

The chemical industry has been one of the principal villains in the spoliation of the English landscape. The details can be found in L. F. Haber, *The Chemical Industry during the Nineteenth Century* (1958), and in A. and N. L. Clow, *The Chemical Revolution* (1952).

The story of New Lanark is told by Norman Dunhill, in 'The history of New Lanark', *Journal of Industrial Archaeology*, Vol. 1, No. 3, November 1964, and in the article by J. Butt, I. Donnachie and J. R. Hume, 'Robert Owen of New Lanark', *Industrial Archaeology*, Vol. 8, No. 2, May 1971.

For the more recent history of brickmaking, the principal published sources are Richard Hillier, *Clay That Burns: a History of the Fletton Brick Industry* (1981); Alan Cox, *Brickmaking: a History and Gazetteer* (1979), and Kenneth Hudson, *Building Materials* (1972). *Bedfordshire Brickfield*, published by the Bedfordshire County Planning Office in 1967, is a detailed description of the area as it was at that time, and makes proposals for reclamation. It is one of the classic post-war studies of industrial dereliction.

The twentieth-century industries have so far been very inadequately covered from an archaeological point of view. The general pattern can be studied in Kenneth Hudson, *The Archaeology of the Consumer Society: the Second Industrial Revolution in Britain* (1983). For the motor industry, H. G. Castle, *Britain's Motor Industry* (1950) is helpful, and so is P. W. Andrews and E. Brunner, *The Life of Lord Nuffield* (1955), although any archaeological information is incidental in both books. On the subject of film studios, C. Oakley, *Where We Came In: the Story of the British Cinematograph Industry* (1964) has most to offer.

Aviation historians have, almost without exception, concentrated on aeroplanes and have very little to say about airports or airfields. Information regarding these strangely neglected aspects of the subject can, however, be pieced together from H. J. Penrose's two books, *British Aviation: the Pioneering Years* (1967), and *British Aviation: the Adventurous Years* (1973). Airports received more attention in Kenneth Hudson and Julian Pettifer, *Diamonds in the Sky: a Social History of Air Travel* (1979).

The best books on industrial housing are Stanley Chapman's *The History of Working-Class Housing* (1971), and J. N. Tann, *Working-Class Housing in Nineteenth-Century Britain* (1971).

Index